FROM SCIENCE
TO FAITH

FROM SCIENCE TO FAITH

Using a Scientific Approach to Strengthen Faith

DR. ADRIEN CHAUVET

KUBE
PUBLISHING

From Science to Faith: Using a scientific approach to strengthen faith

First published in England by
Kube Publishing Ltd
Markfield Conference Centre,
Ratby Lane, Markfield,
Leicestershire, LE67 9SY,
United Kingdom
Tel: +44 (0) 1530 249230
Email: info@ kubepublishing.com
Website: www.kubepublishing.com

The right of Dr Adrien Chauvet to be identified as the
author and translator of this work has been asserted by him
in accordance with the Copyright, Designs and
Patents Act, 1988.

CIP data for this book is available from the British Library.

ISBN: 978-1-84774-195-0 paperback
ISBN: 978-1-84774-196-7 ebook

Cover Design by Inspiral Design
Typesetting by nqaddoura@hotmail.com
Printed by Imak Offset, Turkey

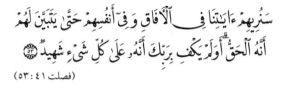

بِسْمِ اللَّهِ الرَّحْمَٰنِ الرَّحِيمِ

سَنُرِيهِمْ ءَايَٰتِنَا فِى ٱلْآفَاقِ وَفِىٓ أَنفُسِهِمْ حَتَّىٰ يَتَبَيَّنَ لَهُمْ
أَنَّهُ ٱلْحَقُّ أَوَلَمْ يَكْفِ بِرَبِّكَ أَنَّهُۥ عَلَىٰ كُلِّ شَىْءٍ شَهِيدٌ ۝

(فصلت ٤١ : ٥٣)

*We will show them Our signs in the horizons
and within themselves until it becomes clear to
them that it is the truth. But is it not sufficient
concerning your Lord that He is, over all things,
a Witness? (Ḥā'. Mīm. al-Sajdah 41:53)*

CONTENTS

TRANSLITERATION TABLE

꧁꧂

Arabic Consonants

Initial, unexpressed medial and final: ʾ ʿ

ا	a	د	d	ض	ḍ	ك	k
ب	b	ذ	dh	ط	ṭ	ل	l
ت	t	ر	r	ظ	ẓ	م	m
ث	th	ز	z	ع	ʿ	ن	n
ج	j	س	s	غ	gh	هـ	h
ح	ḥ	ش	sh	ف	f	و	w
خ	kh	ص	ṣ	ق	q	ي	y

Vowels, diphthongs, etc.

Short:	◌َ a	◌ِ i	◌ُ u
Long:	◌َا ā	◌ِي ī	◌ُو ū
Diphthongs:		◌َوْ aw	
		◌َىْ ay	

INTRODUCTION

My life-long goal has always been to seek meaning in this world, my place within it, and the path I must take. In this pursuit, I essentially seek inner peace, which my travails have come to indicate comes from Truth. By 'Truth' I mean a conception of the world that is logical, practical and universal—encompassing all disciplines and beings. I hope that this Truth will give me the satisfaction of having made the right choice, and of being on the right path. And since I doubt that I am the only one looking for this kind of reassurance, I am sharing my experiences here.

Since a young age, I was immersed in the world of so-called 'hard' sciences: mathematics, physics, chemistry and biology. This socialization was initiated by the scientists and teachers in my family. This admiration for the sciences was then nurtured and reinforced in school, where I was acquainted with formal physics, chemistry and biology.

Through these studies I learned about the material world and about its governing laws. But my background is far from being devoid of religiosity. I come from a place where the church's campanile towers above all the other houses in town, and where chapels and stone crosses are scattered throughout the surrounding hills. I was understandably raised as a practising Christian, going to church twice a week and occasionally serving as the altar boy. However, besides the context of the church, religion was never made relevant in my every-day life. These monuments and rituals were only vestiges of a past that was made obsolete by science. Indeed, with modern sciences being in direct conflict with some Christian texts, when taken literally, I quickly left aside all religious practice and opted for a type of agnosticism. Religious morality and norms were still part of my mindset, but when it came to making sense of this world, I was conditioned to make science prevail over all other conceptual frameworks.

On the way to becoming a scientist, I realized that science was not as 'hard' as I initially thought it was. During these period of study, I also had the chance to travel and discover various cultures and mentalities. Interestingly, out of all my experiences, only spirituality has allowed me to achieve a peace of mind and a sense of satisfaction that transcends the challenges of this life in a way that is lasting and all-encompassing. It is only during my post-graduate studies that I was invited to Islam. I was attracted by its apparent logic and practicality. Soon after my conversion, I had the opportunity to learn about the different aspects of this religion alongside local and international scholars, through private lessons, public lectures and various scholarly and recreational travels. I discovered in Islam a much more convincing and practical philosophy of life that was not in apparent conflict with my scientific background. As a result of my upbringing, I had never put aside this love for science and I naturally decided to continue this spiritual journey in harmony with a certain scientific rationale. More specifically, I sought to use this scientific rationale to validate my spiritual quest.

While my religious studies were marked by spirituality, my scientific studies were instilled with materiality. Unfortunately, many people around me have set these two notions at odds with each other by associating materiality with reason and spirituality with irrationality. Often times, materiality and spirituality end in opposition to each other to the point of becoming contradictory. Nowadays, believing without having material evidence is absurd. Moreover, in the academic world, religion disturbs; it is synonymous with irrationality, manipulation, being old-fashioned and backwardness. Materialistic ideology, on the other hand, is of greater value because it is founded on purely scientific grounds. Indeed, why should one accept the constraint of an ideology that is more than 1,400 years old and follow practices in the name of a God whose existence cannot be scientifically evaluated? The secular discourse of today's societies is essentially fuelled by scientific advances used to discredit the existence of a superior entity. Broadly speaking, materialistic societies reject anything that cannot be measured by physical instruments. They reject anything that cannot be 'datafied'. Whether it is a matter of palaeontology, genetics, astrophysics, chemistry, or other sciences, all the arguments and demonstrations lead one to believe that these so-called exact or hard sciences are worth much more than religious teachings, especially if one's life choices depend on them.

To illustrate this opposition, let me narrate an experience I had during a visit to the University of Zurich, one of the leading research institutes in Europe. It was in 2014, and it happened between two presentations of the *Swiss Chemical Society*. While I was walking across the Irchel campus and I had stopped in front of a small anthropology museum. The museum's primary function was to illustrate the evolution of the human species through about twenty thematic displays. To my surprise, the first display quoted a passage from the Bible stating that the world was only 6,000 years old. This sentence was then ridiculed by contemporary scientific discourse. With implicit and abusive generalizations, the message was clear: the goal was to discredit religious views and show that the secular vision of the world is based on sound and objective scientific facts. A few metres further down the exhibit, the second display proposed a genealogical tree of the human species. It explicitly showed, by means of lighted pathways, that after each discovery of ancient human skeletons, this tree had to be entirely remodelled about a dozen times during the last century! A question naturally came to my mind: how on earth would such "scientific facts" be less illusory than religious texts when both are subjected to the same aleatory interpretations?

The evolution of the human species is only one example, but the opposition between science and religion is noticeable in all aspects of society. Whether it is through the radio broadcasts, newspapers or school curricula, one is constantly challenged to maintain the prevalence of the scientific over the religious and the material over the spiritual. It is therefore no wonder that many of my classmates choose not to believe in God as an outcome of their scientific studies. However, I argue that I found in Islam a logical and practical guide that allows me to follow a rational path on the spiritual land and achieve inner peace.

I thus hope to correct this apparent opposition between scientific and religious thinking. My goal is not to prove scientifically that God exists—at least not directly—but to demonstrate that scientific logic is not foreign to religious logic. Rather, I shed some light on their complementarity and justify, using scientific methods and arguments, a theistic vision of the world. Pursuing this aim, I share in the first chapter a few of the introspective steps that I used to start this journey. The goal is to agree on definitions and a frame of reference that helped me go beyond my comfort zone. In the second chapter I demystify science as it is perceived today. Through a series of examples drawn from my own experiences, I expose the limits of science. The goal of this chapter is helping one to not fall prey to the current scientific dogma. I refer to scientific notions that I have simplified in order to make them accessible to the non-specialists. Technical details are left in footnotes to satisfy the more curious. The third chapter is concerned with the establishment of a scientific theory and its requirements. I then compare these requirements to those that form the basis of faith, Islamically speaking. By comparing the two modes of thinking, the goal is to underline the rationality of the Islamic faith. It is in this chapter that I justify and describe an Islamic vision of the world. Consequently, the language used is framed to assume the truth of Muhammad ﷺ as a Prophet. His name is followed by the honourable mention "ﷺ," which means "May God's peace and blessings be upon him." Likewise, the mention of every other Prophet is followed by "ﷺ" which means "Peace be upon him," and that of the Companions of the Prophet ﷺ are followed by "ﷺ," which means "May God be pleased with him." Some passages in this chapter also include extensive footnotes, which give the reader the choice to hover over or delve into the details of the arguments presented. I however encourage whoever is compelled by the so-called "scientific miracle of the Qur'an" to read them carefully, as they address some common misconceptions. In the fourth chapter, I discuss the limits of purely materialist thinking. The goal is to keep a harmony between the brain and the heart, the intellect and sentience, in one's path to God. Finally, I have kept in an appendix a more detailed discussion about the theory of evolution which assesses both the scientific arguments and the religious texts.

With regard to the Qur'anic passages, I based all translations on Ṣaḥīḥ International. All verses are referenced according to the Uthmanic codex. Regarding the prophetic narrations, they are referenced according to the electronic classification of the USC-MSA. Given the universal nature of the arguments in Chapters I, II and IV, this text is addressed to whoever is in search of spirituality, whatever their belief. It is only in Chapter III that I justify an Islamic worldview, which implicitly leaves the followers of all other denominations the duty to justify their own beliefs. My goal is not to impose a vision of the world, but to propose one that I find appealing and then proceed to discuss it.

I

THE FIRST STEPS IN MY
SPIRITUAL QUEST

❧⸱⸱❧

As a scientist, I was faced with the question of determining the facts that could prove the existence of God and justify adherence to a specific religion. This question prompted me to look for proofs and justifications and undertake a quest for truth. I embarked on this journey more than a decade ago by questioning my own conceptions, norms and cultural practices and evaluating new ones. In this chapter I enumerate the different intellectual positions that allowed me to undertake this journey.

1. Looking beyond materiality

As I was raised in an ultra-capitalist society (ultra, given the number of toys I had), I was naturally tempted to value what brings me the most benefit, whether material or psychological. However, all material benefits derived from people, practices or ideologies ended up disappointing me with the passage of time because they inevitably wane: bodies age, objects wear out and desires change. By seeking only material pleasures, I thus condemned myself to be continually dissatisfied. Consequently, my quest could not confine itself to a mere search for materiality but rather focus on the psychological well-being that the material world provides. For example, an athlete who competes in a championship wants to see his or her efforts validated by a medal. Since the medal can be bought in a specialised store, what the athlete is looking for is not the medal itself, but what it represents and the feeling it provides, namely, success in a competition and the appreciation of others. To achieve this sense of satisfaction, the athlete is ready to go through considerable sacrifices: dietary restrictions, intensive training and high-level competition.

The next step is to choose what psychological pleasure would benefit me the most. For example, I can derive pleasure from eating a sweet but will suffer from its side effects. If I am looking for an ever-lasting pleasure, then I should seek to derive it from something that is not only uncircumscribed by people or materiality but also ever-lasting, such as truth. Assuming that truth is constant and absolute, it becomes a source of security and permanent satisfaction: to do the "right thing" is satisfying, it soothes and gives confidence. As a scientist, I have this feeling of satisfaction, for example, when I find the solution to a maths problem after many attempts or when I finally understand an abstract notion of physics. The feeling of satisfaction therefore follows after exerting a measure of effort, whether physical or intellectual. I therefore assume that the noblest and most lasting satisfaction lies in this quest for truth. And, like a high-level athlete, I must dare to put aside some of the immediate material pleasures for the purpose of striving for higher objectives; to make an effort and invest in a potentially better future.

2. Being aware of the circles of influence

Once I was ready to make an effort to look for an ultimate Truth, the next step was to find out where my ideas and norms came from, and then dare to question them. For example, current statistics show that a student spends on average three hours per day in school—being schooled—and a bit more than that on social media (including news feeds). Thus, schools and broadcasted news are two leading socialising factors of our times. The issue that arises from growing up within such socialising circles is that most of the acquired information is transmitted to us by a third party. Whether it is through a TV host who reads a text that scrolls before his eyes, or through a teacher who follows a certain curriculum, the reported information is stamped with the perception of the one who transmits it: the chain of transmission between the one who witnesses the act and ourselves can be quite long. Indeed, the broadcasted news come from an unknown reporter whose agenda and ideology are often unknown. Moreover, one does not see what is hidden in the blind spot of the camera. Being positioned on the other side of the screen, with no access to the scene from which images are taken, means the tools at one's disposition for discerning truth from falsehood are limited.

I remember, for example, a high school student who asked me, during a physics lesson, if the magic show she watched on television was 'real magic.' What then of a documentary made abroad? In the absence of a critical sense or alternative points of view, one can only absorb and take as reference what is transmitted. As far as the school curriculum is concerned, it is put together by a national institution that has a pre-established political programme. I, for example, always wondered why my teachers insisted on certain subjects, such as the two world wars, which were reviewed almost every year, and why they were silent about other topics such as colonization, although it has as much impact on today's society.

The goal is thus to question any information that is given to one, or at least to become aware of their implications. Unfortunately, in the absence of counterexamples and critical thinking, the definitions promoted by schools or by the media become one's primary points of reference. In order to overcome one's naivety, the solution would be to verify each and every item of information one receives.

3. Realizing that trust is necessary

Unfortunately, I am unable to verify every piece of information while the rejection of all information that I am unable to verify does not allow me to properly evolve in society. For example, I cannot afford to travel to China to check whether this country and its people really exist, or check whether a researcher in his laboratory has told the whole truth about his data. And yet, China and the researcher's results are necessary for me to understand and evolve in this world. Our life is therefore based on trust. Indeed, there is no need to understand the electronic architecture of a mobile phone in order to be able to use it. One trusts that teachers will transmit the necessary tools to succeed in life; one also trusts that the news channel provides objective information; just as one trusts that the surveillance systems that infiltrate our' lives are used to protect us. From the moment one realises that one does not have direct access to the Truth, because it is temporarily out of reach, one must accept that intellectual development is based on transposed information. The question of trust then becomes central, but how does one acquire this trust? On what basis should one trust? Who and what can be considered a credible source of knowledge? And, most importantly, by what kind of information should one let oneself be influenced?

4. Making rational choices

To trust a specific source of knowledge implies that one has made a choice between all the different sources of knowledge available. As I have been conditioned to think rationally, I therefore choose to put my trust in what seems to be the most logical. To be rational or logical can, for example, mean that my actions coincide with my words. By following this "common sense" rule, it is obvious that any person or institution that trade their moral principles to gain votes or market shares will lose their credibility. To be, scientifically speaking, coherent in my choices also requires me to follow that which has the highest probability of happening, to judge by what is evident and avoid any suspicions and unfounded superstitions. These last conditions require introspection as well as a questioning of one's own cohort. It may be that my closest friend is misled while the person I despise is actually right. In order to adequately choose which person deserves my trust, I first need to learn about that person. Towards this aim, an experience must be shared with this person: either directly, for example, during a road trip or a joint study project, or indirectly, by cross-referencing multiple stories recounting the character of this person. In either case, it is the altruism and consistency taken in given situations that determine one's trustworthiness: the more a person acts in a materially disinterested way, and the more respectful of himself and of those around him, the more I would be inclined to listen to him. In relation to my spiritual quest, if I am looking for a spiritual guide, I will use this principle to choose whose teachings to follow.

5. Walking with harmony

The building of trust and the subsequent choice of a specific teacher also depends on the nature of these teachings: they must make sense, both intellectually and emotionally. Indeed, I have a brain and a heart, an intellect as well as the ability to feel. Both the brain and the heart are part of the same individual. The two faculties must consequently be taken into consideration in order to achieve inner peace. In other words, my spiritual quest will be more relevant if it is justified by my intellect. Instinctively, if there is a conflict between the spiritual and material conceptions of the world, I will assume that one of them is amiss: either my understanding of religious texts is not appropriate, or my scientific reasoning is faulty. More specifically, if both religion and science are describing the same world, and both claim to approach Truth, then I am expecting that they should agree with each other. While trying to reach an agreement, I should not be afraid to question one or the other. Such questioning will be key if I want to elevate myself both spiritually and rationally. Such questioning also implies that doubts might ensue in both the religion and the science I have learned up until that point. But I can be confident that at the end of this journey, harmony between the two will only get stronger, more stable and long-lasting.

6. Chapter summary

My quest for inner peace is premised on introspection. At first, I ought to put aside immediate material satisfaction for a deferred but longer-lasting and more intense pleasure. The second step is to realize the importance of external influences in the shaping of my own self. I then must acknowledge the necessity of trust and choose wisely whom to trust. Intuitively, I put my trust in what is coherent, altruistic and constant. The goal is to undertake this journey while maintaining harmony between rationality and feeling.

II

RE-EVALUATING FAITH IN SCIENCE

❧❧❧

Here I stand, ready to take on this journey toward Truth with the aim of achieving inner peace. In order to fully explore new horizons, other religions or new ideologies, I choose to re-evaluate the basis on which my conception of the world stands. In other words, I am going to re-evaluate, using scientific reasoning, what I used to consider as 'scientific truths.' I posit that this re-evaluation takes place in four stages. First, I think it is necessary to beware of the limits of one's physical abilities as well as the scope of one's current understanding of the world. Second, I show that one can overcome these limitations by using probabilities. Third, from a scientific point of view, I illustrate that a set of probabilities or, more generally, a set of indirect evidence are sufficient to validate an abstract concept, whether it is quantum mechanics or the existence of God. Fourth, I show that the current scientific understanding of the world only demonstrates its exceptionality. In conclusion, I will argue that the idea of the Divine is no more simplistic than an atheistic conception of the universe. On the contrary, the uniqueness of the world can serve as evidence to support a theist worldview.

1. The fringes of our perception

As a human, I perceive my environment through my senses (touch, sight, hearing, etc.), which are naturally restricted. I cannot see through walls, nor hear the footsteps of an ant. Technological advances allow me to overcome these limitations, to push them further and, as a result, help me see new phenomena and boundaries. The following are a few examples to illustrate the limits of our physical laws:

a. *At the frontiers of the extreme*

Scientific theories only describe what we perceive from the world. They are thus contextual in the sense that they evolve as a function of new scientific discoveries. For example, unlike the macroscopic world in which I evolve, the world of the infinitely small is 'quantized.' While a piece of furniture can be placed anywhere in a room, one finds that the electron, for instance, does not accept to be placed at any random place around the atom's nucleus. On the contrary, an electron can only be found in a well-defined state such as energy level, orbit or spin). Another fundamental theory that reshaped the past century is Einstein's theory of general relativity. In agreement with this theory, one finds that time passes faster or slower depending on the speed at which one moves. This new theory compelled scientists to correct the intuitive Newtonian notions that had prevailed until then because they could not explain the phenomena studied at the time. In other words, our theories and physical laws are a function of our awareness of the physical world. Definitions are either refined or changed according to new discoveries. Thus, I must not see physical laws as absolute truths but rather as approximations that allow me to describe what I currently perceive of the world. The laws in place are therefore contextual and I must expect to see them evolving to embrace future discoveries.

b. *The subjective interpretation of objective results*

Regardless of how objective a measurement can be, its interpretation will always be done by a subjective human. Accordingly, scientific enquiry is an intrinsically sub-jective endeavour. For example, analytical tools such as a magnifying glass, microscope, computer or synchrotron, allow one to push the limits of one's abilities and perceptions. But re-gardless of the objectivity of the tools, the conclusion of the analysis will always be given by a subjective scientist. His or her interpretation will thus depend on his or her point of view, training and beliefs. For instance, the study of a molecule cannot be done with the naked eye because it is too small and it moves too fast. The molecule is studied via its spectrum,[1] but to define a molecule's electronic state by means of its spectrum is far from being trivial. The interpretation is often based on mathematical models, which themselves are based on the researcher's expectations. In other words, one's conclusions depend on what one expects to see in this molecule. If one does not understand the result, which is often the case, then one opts for a more complex theoretical model until it coincides with the experimental results. Subjectivity is therefore an integral part of the interpretation of results, and the latter is clothed with objectivity only by the accumulation of arguments that can support it.

c. *The uncertainty principle*

Because I am physically limited, my knowledge of the physical world is also limited. One of the most explicit examples that illustrates the limitations of our knowledge is Heisenberg's 'uncertainty principle.' This principle states that one cannot know simultaneously the exact position and speed of an object. In other words, one must opt to discard one to know the other with greater precision. For example, if one knows the exact position of an electron, then one has no idea of its speed, and therefore of its energy. Alternatively, if one knows the exact energy of an

---

1. The spectrum of a molecule is its ability to absorb certain colours/wavelength. Each electronic state has a specific spectral signature. Consequently, the modulations of this spectrum over time give indications of the successive states occupied by the molecule: ground state, excited state, ionized state, for example.

electron, then one has no idea of where it is at that precise instant. There is in no ways of measuring them both accurately and simultaneously. This partial knowledge shows my inability to grasp the Truth which, in this case, is defined by the exact and simultaneous position and energy of an object.[2]

d. *Section summary*

In summary, our physical laws are but a function of what is materially apparent to us, and only God knows the extent of what is hidden from us. One of the most explicit acknowledgements of our ignorance is the notion of 'dark matter.' This concept emerges from the discrepancy between two different ways to estimated mass of the universe. I turn out that the estimated mass calculated via the trajectories of galaxies is much larger than the estimated mass of the visible content—the sum of all visible galaxies, stars, clouds of gas and dust, to name some elements). This difference indicates that either our theo-

---

2. One could argue that such a principle is only relevant if one accepts in the first place these modern theories. I would then respond that the uncertainty principle is not restricted to the world of the infinitely small, such as electrons, photons, but also applies to large-scale objects. Water waves at the surface of the sea, for example, can be characterized by their frequency, f, or wavelength, λ, (both being related through $v=f.\lambda$, with v being the velocity). The more ripples at the surface of the water, the more defined the frequency, the less defined the position of this wave. Indeed, the wave spreads as far as one can see oscillations at the surface. By contrast, the position of a rogue wave can be clearly determined while its frequency is undefined.

ries are simply wrong, or there exists some 'dark matter' or 'dark energy', which is defined as matter that we are not yet able to perceive and which constitutes more than 95% of the universe. Scientists tend for the second option and believe that we are still unaware of more than 95% of our universe! Either ways, this last example reinforces the idea that our physical laws are only the result of analysis, which are limited by our subjectivity, knowledge and understanding. Physical laws thus cannot be taken as absolute truths, but rather as contextual explanations.

2. Advancing despite our restrictions

When I cannot solve equations, whether because of my lack of knowledge (insufficient data) or lack of ability (being unable to process all data), I can always resort to approximations or probabilities. I must therefore accept to take what is most probable as being closer to the Truth. I will now illustrate the use of probability in our life through some examples.

a. *Fluctuation and statistical averages*

Statistics are central in the development of financial in-stitutions. In particular, when we look at the stock market, he who can predict the evolution of the market is guaranteed to prosper financially. Stock market predictions are based on multiple factors, including past prices, price of related items, social trends, political moves, among others. However, knowing and taking each of these data into account is impossible because of their sheer numbers and complex interdependency. To overcome this obstacle, the common trader can establish averages and look for recurring patterns. One then flies over the details to predict general trends and base one's choices on the prediction that is most likely to occur.

b. *Weather forecasts*

One of the objectives of probabilities is to predict future events. Past experiences allow one to establish trends and see patterns which are then put into equations. Weather forecast is one example: according to current conditions, such as wind speed and direction, temperature, and humidity, etc., one can use computational modelling to predict what the weather will be. But the current calculations, which already make use of the most powerful supercomputers, still cannot take into account every single factor. Thus, one makes use of approximations, such as replacing small and dispersed clouds by an overall higher humidity index. Although the results are mere approximations, they are as close to the Truth as it can be as far as the weather is concerned. The usefulness of probabilities in that example is obvious, and it is common practice to base one's life choices on them.

c. *The wavefunction*

Probabilities also dictate the ways through which we un-der-stand the basic mechanisms of life. From a materialist point of view, life is an intricate succession of chemical reactions that take place between molecules. The fundamental building blocks of molecules are atoms, and a key characteristic of molecules and atoms are their electronic configuration. By electronic configuration, I mean the state of electrons around the nuclei. This electronic configuration is given by the wavefunction. Although the wavefunction is a specific mathematical formula, its application only results in probabilities. Indeed, when trying to find solutions for the configuration of electrons, the wavefunction only indicates the location where electrons are most likely to be found. Even though the solutions are not exact, these informed guesses allow one to predict the overall shapes of atomic orbitals. Consequently, this allows one to better understand how atoms join together to form molecules, and how these molecules interact with each other. This theory forms the base of modern chemistry, which is so far successful.

d. *Section summary*

In summary, probabilities do not provide an absolute Truth, but in the absence of more precise knowledge, approximations are the only tool in one's hand for attempting to understand the world. One must therefore accept the highest probability available as representing what is closest to the Truth. This reliance on highest probabilities is key in establishing scientific theories, and advancing human understanding and control of the world. Similarly, probabilities can be key in the establishment of faith in

God as well as in justifying an Islamic conception of the world, as I will discussed in the following chapters.

3. Believing in the unseen

One learns about the world through the senses and also through the tools one possesses. The perception of the outside world is the proof of its existence. However, most of the time, one cannot see, taste, touch, feel or hear directly certain objects whose existence is perceived only through indirect means. Such indirect experiences are in many cases sufficient to establish a conviction. below I will enumerate some examples of established scientific concepts that solely rely on indirect evidence.

a. *The electron*

As common as they are, no one has ever seen electrons as only their effects can be seen. When one sees a lightning bolt in the sky or the spark of the gas igniter, one sees the light that is emitted as a result of the passage of electrons, not the electrons themselves.[3] In the same way, when using electric appliances, one sees only the consequence of the passage of electrons: the motor turns, light is emitted or the stove heats up. One can only feel electrons indirectly,

---

3. In an electric arc, electrons move from air molecules to air molecules while exciting them. When a molecule is excited, it promotes its own electrons to higher energy levels and can even loose some of them. When the electron relaxes or recombine with its host molecule, it releases its extra energy by emitting light, which forms the arc we see.

by being electrocuted for example, or by measuring the current they produce. Although, it is accepted that electrons cannot be directly perceived, no one dares denying that these electrons exist and that they are constituents of each and every atom. Once considered as the product of an obscure theory, today their existence is not even questioned. It is in fact the increasing use of and reference to the electron's theory that reinforces one's conviction that electrons do exist.

b. *Electromagnetic waves*

Electromagnetic waves are one of the abstract physical notions that help make sense of the world. In particular, they are used to describe light and even radio waves. The human body is only sensitive to a certain range of electromagnetic waves. While the spectrum of light is theoretically infinite,[4] the eye, for instance, only perceives a restricted colour range, between 400 nm (blue) and 800 nm (red), which is called visible light. Another common type of light is infrared light, which is produced, for example, by the sun, incandescent bulbs, and oven plates. Although the eye does not see this infrared light, one feels the heat it generates. Other waves, like radio waves or microwaves, go through one's body without being seen or felt. But as long as the radio, satellite and mobile phone work, the

---

4. Light can be thought of as an electromagnetic wave whose spectrum extends from X-rays to ultra-violet, visible light, infra-red, microwaves, radio waves etc.

existence of these waves is undisputed. Interestingly, light can also be seen as a photon, which is a particle-like well-defined amount of energy. This dual nature of light shows that talking about electromagnetic waves is simply one of the ways that is used to conceptualize light and its interaction with objects.

c. *Forces*

Forces also are mere conceptions. By forces I, for example, refer to the electric, magnetic (i.e. electromagnetic) and gravitational forces that govern the universe.. Forces are used to describe and explain the interactions between objects, but they remain a vision, or an interpretation, of these interactions. Indeed, these forces cannot be seen directly. The concept of force is only a mathematical tool, a formula, an arrow on a sheet of paper, but it helps explain the world and make better sense of it. The value of a theory like this is decided by its usefulness. Thus, it is through its utility and applicability that a theory is accepted as being more or less close to the Truth.

d. *Section summary*

In short, from a scientific point of view, the impossibility to directly and physically perceive something is not proof that it does not exist. All the above examples refer to scientific concepts that are solely based on indirect proof, also called evidences. Evidence is inherently subject to interpretations. The accumulation of evidence that supports itself as well as the utility of a theory provide a sufficient argument to validate said theory. I can now use the same scientific reasoning and apply it to the realm of faith: evidences, or indirect proofs, are equally sufficient to make the case for the existence of God. When taken individually, each evidence is justifiably subject to multiple interpretations, but when taken together, it is enough that the evidence supports itself and fits a specific theist conception of the world. I will discuss the 'fitting conditions' in the next chapter. For now, I want to emphasize that I do not need to see God, nor do I need to witness unprecedented or unexplained phenomena to believe in God. I am allowed, following the same scientific rational, to base my faith in God on a set of evidence.

4. The natural argument

In this section, I will enumerate some scientific arguments that, as a scientist, I found particularly appealing to justify the existence of God, or more generally, of a higher entity that engendered and governs this world. As mentioned in the introduction, my goal is not to prove God by means of an absolute, irrefutable argument, but simply to show that believing in Him is scientifically justifiable. Among the several types of arguments that have been used over the centuries to justify the existence of God, the one I adhere to most is the so-called 'natural' argument. The natural argument consists in showing that the singularity and precision of the natural world point to the existence of a higher power. The goal is not to rely on God for what I cannot understand, but to appreciate the world's exceptionality. It is then up to each individual to decide which explanation, God or randomness, is better suited to explain this exceptionality.

a. *Complexification of life*

To start with the most obvious example, I first want to talk about the exceptionality of life. Life in itself is exceptional, in the sense that scientists still wonder how life could possibly emerge from inanimate matter. Indeed, a living organism is like an ensemble of precisely interlocked pieces of machinery that work together not only to sustain the whole, but also to multiply and complexify it. However, from experience, everything else, besides living organisms, tends to a greater disorder. In school I was taught that disorder, called entropy, can only spontaneously increase, like when one pours ink in water, and as a result, they irreversibly mix. Everything tends to reach the lowest energy level, or the most stable configuration. For example, if marbles are left to roll on the ground, they are subject to earth's gravitation. They will roll to the lowest point available, which lowers their (potential) energy and provides stability. Speaking of energy, I also learned that nothing is lost, nothing is created, but that energy is only transmitted and transformed. I would argue that above all, energy is dissipated through friction and radiation. It is remarkable that biological life in itself goes against this law of disorder as each organism evolves and develops. In some ways, life challenges this process of homogenization. Indeed, the organism's reproduction, metabolism, and physical development tend to complexify and segregate rather than simplify and randomize. Life is therefore exceptional in and of itself. By exceptional, I mean a phenomenon that goes against all expectations based on common logic; a phenomenon whose probability of occurrence is insignificant. One must keep in mind that the aforementioned complexification is only made possible by the sun. All forms of earthy life (past and present) are directly or indirectly connected to the use of solar radiation: the greenhouse effect the trapping of solar radiation by our atmosphere—provides living creatures with an average temperature that allows for liquid water. This liquid water enables vegetal life via photosynthesis. The sun is thus the primary energy source of plants, on which animals feed. Up to this day, humans are burning fossil fuels (coal, petrol, gas) that were once living organisms nurtured by the sun. The Earth only intercepts a tiny portion of radiations that are emitted by the sun. It is as if the solar radiations are a stream of water and the Earth is a tiny cup with which one collects some of the water. Humans are thus bathing in an inexhaustible flux of energy (within their human scale of space and time). By utilising this flow of solar energy, life correspond to an exceptionally intricate use of this energy, that is so far unique in the universe. Life thus represents an apparent exception to this law of homogenization because of the unusual way homogenization take place. Just like the mill, which uses a small portion of the river to turn its wheel: the flow of water represents here the flow of solar energy, and the spinning gears of the mill correspond to life on earth. Based on current scientific comprehension of the world, the probability of finding such gears 'by chance' borders more on science fiction than genuine science. But like any other hypothesis that the human mind can formulate, it deserves to be evaluated. I refer here to the theory of evolution, which will be discussed in an appendix. The argument I make is that, even from an evolutionist point of view, human existence finds its origins in a combination of circumstances that defies all expectations. It is thus natural to wonder whether humans are the effect of a combination of mere random circumstances or the result of a Divine orchestration. The point is not to rely on God for what we cannot understand, but to appreciate the exceptionality of life, and take it as a sign that points toward a greater orchestrator.

b. *Unique living conditions*

After having discussed the exceptionality of life, I discuss here the exceptional conditions that allows life to strive. Indeed, the Earth plays the role of a unique type of cradle. I mentioned earlier that life, as we know it, requires energy from the sun. But more importantly, life requires liquid water in sufficient quantity, to enable the necessary chemistry of life. A planet too small would not have enough atmosphere to keep its water in the liquid phase. Indeed, water would simply evaporate in thin atmospheres, as it is the case for the moon. A planet without an active core would not allow the degassing of the mantel nor allow accumulation of the degassed water at the surface. Indeed, without the protective magnetic field provided by an active core, surface water would become ionized and blown away by solar winds, as it is the case for Mars. Similarly, a planet that is too close to the sun, like Mercury, or too far away, like Pluto, would see its surface water either being evaporated or frozen because their temperatures are either too high or too low. The rotation of the Earth, its atmosphere, its active core, its distance from the sun, the size of its warm body, etc. give the Earth an almost constant temperature over the years. Plus-minus forty degrees celsius, from winter to summer, is a variation that can be considered negligible compared to the few thousand degrees of the sun and the almost absolute zero of space. Furthermore, this almost constant temperature ideally sits in the tiny range where water is liquid. For comparison, let us represent temperature on a ruler with the absolute zero on one end and the Sun's surface near the 5.8-metres mark (i.e. corresponding to ~5800-degree Kelvin). We are here talking about a variation of +/- 4 cm (i.e. corresponding to +/- 40 degrees) ideally placed within a 10 cm-wide range where water is found in a liquid state—corresponding to the 100 degree range between the freezing and boiling point of water. Outside that 10 cm range, water is either frozen, thus too stiff to facilitate any chemical reactions, or vaporized, and thus not dense enough to enable the chemical reactions required for life. The temperature on Earth allows for most of this surface water to be kept in its liquid phase for periods of times that are long enough to allow life and its development.

To appreciate how exceptional Earth is, I also like to follow the scientific search for exoplanets, and more specifically the ones that are similar to Earth. Despite the (literally) astronomical efforts of researchers to scrutinize the universe, the number of planets whose conditions are potentially similar to Earth is confined to a few thousand planets.[5] This number will certainly increase with the development of new spectroscopic techniques. However, as the closest of these planets is located light years away from Earth, their confirmation is solely based on indirect observations and theoretical models.[6] So far, the latest space explorations reinforce the idea that the Earth's environment is unique: our solar system is located in a very particular branch of our galaxy that is not subject to devastating supernovae explosions.[7] The Earth has a magnetic field that protects humans, animals and plants from life-threatening solar winds and has a composition that is neither harmful

---

5. Among around 4000 candidates in 2020, the NASA has reported that "K2-18b is the only exoplanet known to have both water and temperatures that could support life." Unfortunately, "given the high level of activity of its red dwarf star, K2-18b may be more hostile to life as we know it than Earth, as it is likely to be exposed to more high-energy radiation." In other words, to this day, we don't know about any other planets that have similar environment and conditions like our Earth. (https://www.nasa.gov/feature/goddard/2019/nasa-s-hubble-finds-water-vapor-on-habitable-zone-exoplanet-for-1st-time)

6. For the detection methods of exoplanets, see: J.T. Wright (2017). Radial Velocities as an Exoplanet Discovery Method. arXiv:170 7.07983 [astro-ph.EP]

    For the methods of trace-life detection, see: E.W. Schwieterman *et al.* (2017). Exoplanet Biosignatures: A Review of Remotely Detectable Signs of Life. arXiv: 1705.05791 [astro-ph.EP]

7. C.H. Lineweaver *et al.* (2004). The Galactic Habitable Zone and the Age Distribution of Complex Life in the Milky Way. *Science*, Vol. 303, DOI: 10.1126/science.1092322

(by an excess of chemical components unfit for life such as acids, sulphur compounds, oxidants, to name a few), nor sterile[8] (by a lack of elements necessary for life such as carbon, nitrogen, oxygen, hydrogen, iron, magnesium, etc.). It is the combination of all these necessary conditions that enables life and preserve it, which shows the uniqueness of Earth. It is as if Earth was specifically designed for the development of life. I therefore stand close to those who argue for 'the fine tuning of the universe.'[9] in the sense that it is the extreme degree of precision required in the laws of nature, which allows the development of life as we know it, that makes me marvel. It is the exceptionality of each of these conditions and the ways they combine that turn my eyes towards the possibility of a guided creation instead of a world that has emerged from randomness and left to itself.

---

8. See in particular Section 6 entitled "Factors for Continuous Planetary Habitability," in C.S Cockell *et al.* (2016). Habitability: A Review. *Astrobiology*, Vol. 16, DOI: 10.1089/ast.2015.1295

9. The argument of the *Fine tuning of the universe* is the argument which highlights that a tiny variation of the constants of the world would engender its collapse. See the Stanford Philosophical Encyclopaedia for a more elaborate definition and discussion (*https://plato.stanford. edu/entries/fine-tuning/*). This position is not to be confused with the *Intelligent Design* argument, which seeks to find justifications for the existence of God in scientific wonders. Although both ask one to marvel at the world, the later starts with the assumption that God exists in the first place, while the former simply points out the exceptionality of the world but does not make any claims regarding a Divine orchestration. It is only once one accepts a religious worldview that the whole material world and its governing laws become a Divine manifestation.

c. *Photosynthesis at the origin of life*

After touching on the exceptionality of life and the Earth as a cradle for life, I now want to talk about a subject that is probably less known to the non-scientific community, but which is certainly as exceptional: photosynthesis. Indeed, one does not have to look to the horizons of our universe to find marvels of organization and fine-tuned processes. Similar marvels are found in the weeds that one steps on and which are considered as nuisances. These weeds, like any other plants, derive their energy from a process called photosynthesis: the process by which solar energy is converted into chemical energy. I studied photosynthesis in my early postgraduate years. The entire plant kingdom as well as some bacteria use this mechanism to live, grow and multiply. One of the consequences of photosynthesis is the production of atmospheric oxygen. The process itself involves a series of small colourful molecules (chlorophylls) which are organized in such a way that they absorb sunlight and transmit this energy to one another until it releases a high-energy electron. These electrons are then used to pump protons across the plant's membrane, whichgenerates an electrochemical gradient. This cellular membrane, which acts as a dam that keeps protons from flowing through to reach equilibrium, can thus be equated to a battery with its positive and negative sides. This biological battery ultimately drives the production of a universal biological energy currency called ATP.[10]

---

10. J.F. Allen (2002). Photosynthesis of ATP - Electrons, Proton Pumps, Rotors, and Poise. *Cell*, Vol. 110, pp. 273-276.

Focussing on the first few steps, the different molecules involved in the capture of solar energy as well as in the release and transport of the electron are all maintained in a protein matrix called the Reaction Centre. Interestingly, one finds the same core structure of this machinery in all photosynthetic organisms without exception.[11] By as-suming that each species has developed from a previous one, inheriting some of its characteristics, one comes to the conclusion that this Reaction Centre, as sophisticated as it may be, was already present in the earliest forms of life. This is because the first form of life is believed to be photosynthetic. In conclusion, this Reaction Centre, with its complex molecular structure, must have been fully operational more than three billion years ago![12]

Although this Reaction Centre must have existed as a complete functioning engine from the start, certain of its properties have evolved over time. But the overall core structure and principle remained the same. To imagine that such Reaction Centre can appear by chance is like disassembling a two-stroke engine, putting all the bits in a bag and hoping that, after shaking it well enough, the engine would re-assemble itself.

I would further add that this machinery does not rely on the random assembly of amino acids. The Reaction Centre is a dimer, meaning that it consists of a doublet

---

11. R.E. Blankenship (2010). Early Evolution of Photosynthesis. *Plant Physiol.*, Vol. 154, pp. 434-438.

12. *Cf.* note 11.

of each constituent protein. The probability of finding one protein of each is already low, but the probability of finding two that meet and assemble before one or the other deteriorates indicates the need for a mass production of such proteins. Currently, the only biological process known to accurately create multiple copies of identical protein is the one which involves the coding of genetic material (DNA or RNA). Molecular coding comes with all the associated molecular machinery that is necessary to maintain the genetic code, decode it and then translate it into proteins. Even more interesting is the fact that this biological engine, like the combustion engine, does not work on its own. To be functional, it needs to be implanted in a membrane and be surrounded by a series of other proteins that provide and collect the electrons and protons it pumps across the membrane, so that it does not get blocked. It also requires a series of proteins capable of using the potential gradient once generated (such as ATP synthetase). In other words, the first Reaction Centre needed a fully functional biological system to preserve its design and use it appropriately. In short, scientists, including evolutionists, are not yet able to rationally explain the origin of life. I mention this not to say that it is impossible, or that it will never be explained in scientific terms, but only to point out the fiction behind the current scientific discourse. Here again, in light of photosynthesis' precision and omnipresence within the vegetal kingdom, my mind naturally turns towards a Grand Orchestrator.

d. *Section summary*

It is through the observation of the world around and within us that the singularity of this universe becomes apparent, life itself being the most striking element of this singularity. Probably because this fauna and flora seem omnipresent in temperate climate countries, this singularity of life has lost its exceptionality and seem to be the norm. Thanks to the intellectual efforts of scientists who are in constant pursuit of a better understanding of the universe, one is able to appreciate life and its exceptionality anew. However, as mentioned initially, these wonders are but evidences. They are not absolute proof of God. The evidence allows for both theist and atheist interpretations. The fact that the scientific community is made of both believers and atheists or, should I say, naturalists, shows that the beauty, complexity and balance of the world are not categorical proofs for the existence or non-existence of God. It is thus left to each person to evaluate the explanation that seems most likely, logical and useful.

5. Chapter summary

To conclude, science should not be embraced as a dogma but rather as a perception, a point of view, a possible explanation of the world. One must keep in mind the limits of human perception and consequently the limits of physical laws. The limitation of human perceptions is fortunately not an obstacle to human development: probabilities and statistics, for example, illustrate well how these limits can be overcome. In the absence of direct and categorical proofs, one has to base their conclusions on incomplete data, uncertain results and what seems to be closest to 'Truth'. Indeed, the establishment of a scientific law can rely on a combination of indirect experiences. Similarly, in order to prove the existence of God it is not necessary to feel Him by touch or sight, for example Recognizing God indirectly in His creation is sufficient to strengthen faith in Him. When I deal with the question of the existence of God or, more generally, the existence of a superior entity which orchestrates this universe, I must evaluate each hypothesis: am I the result of a Divine will or of randomness governed by self-sustaining natural laws? Both hypotheses can be subject to bias, and neither can be directly supported or refuted by material proofs. It is the duty of each person to adjust the graduation of the balance: God on the one hand, and His absence, on the other. One can then put on each pan the evidences that support one or the other; the needle of the balance wavers from one side to the other according to the weight given to each of these evidences. By listing in this chapter a series of scientific wonders, the goal is not to simply fill the gaps of knowledge with God and force onto the reader a theist view of the world. The goal is to show that, given the extent of current scientific knowledge and the demonstrated exceptionality of our world, the idea of a superior being is not as fictional as the current atheist perception of the world purports it to be.

III

THE ISLAMIC PARADIGM

I n this chapter I explore the common elements between science and religion in order to justify, using a scientific rationale, the Islamic worldview, which I call the Islamic paradigm. The first step in this discussion is to define what a scientific paradigm is and what are its implications. In brief, a scientific paradigm is to see the world through scientific lenses. To live in a scientific paradigm is to live in a world that is primarily informed by science. And accordingly, as science evolves, the paradigm also evolves. In other words, current scientific paradigms are governed by the scientific theories that are currently held to be true. But one is not bound to live by science. For example, religiously-oriented people live according to a religious paradigm. And while scientific paradigms are informed by scientific theories, religious paradigms, at least in the three Abrahamic religions, are informed by Revelation. The goal of this chapter is then to compare the establishment and, thus, the validity of each of these two paradigms. The goal is not to discredit one in favour of the other, because I don't necessarily hold them as being mutually exclusive, but to highlight the similarities between the two. I admit that, while scientific theories are man-made explanations of observed phenomena, religion is based on Revelation. But even if the production of knowledge in the two differs, both religion and science try to make sense of the same world. They both help explain human presence on Earth. They both help explain and interpret the events that take place in human life. On one hand, natural sciences enlightens one about the mechanisms of life and allows one to anticipate the material consequences of one's actions. Religion, on the other hand, describes the immaterial consequences of one's actions. In this regard, both science and religion guide one's decisions.

Furthermore, once the scientist has established his theory based on his observations, and once the theologian has established his understanding of the revealed texts, the methodologies and conditions for accepting either worldviews are intrinsically similar. I go so far as to argue that the thought process that allows me to accept a scientific theory is the same as the thought process required to accept a religious view of the world. It is therefore in light of these common elements that I evaluate the Islamic paradigm in the same way as I would evaluate any other scientific paradigms. I thus begin this chapter by enumerating the core criteria used to establish a scientific paradigm and, more specifically, a scientific theory: its origin, relevance and benefits. I then pursue with an evaluation of Islam according to the same scientific rational.

1. The establishment of a scientific theory

From a scientific point of view, a theory is a set of rules and concepts which explain observed phenomena. The scientific value of a theory lies in its ability to describe and predict events in this world. However, if one also takes into account the social aspect that contributes to the establishment of a theory and to its public recognition, then one must also take into account the author as well as the usefulness of the theory. This chapter therefore discusses the three main factors required to establish a theory: its origin, relevance and utility.

a. *Origin*

From a logical point of view, the validity of a theory should be independent of the person who proposes it. However, experience shows that the status of this person and his context are critical for promoting his theory, especially when it proposes a marginal vision of the world. Indeed, anyone can theorize about anything. But, as stated in the first chapter, a theory is taken seriously only if it comes from a reliable and respected source of knowledge. In particular, the more a person is versed in the science in which he theorizes, the more trusted his opinion will be. Similarly, a theory would be swiftly accepted when it validates other pre-established notions. The theory of special relativity, for example, was ignored by much of the British, French and American scientific community during the decade following its publication in 1905. The theory was initially devalued either because it did not hold account of the popular theory of ether, because it provided no immediate material benefit, or because it was simply not understood.[13] It was indeed the diligence of Einstein and the constructive criticism of his German colleagues that progressively forced the rest of the scientific community to take it into consideration. One could argue that truth will prevail regardless of its origin. In other words, even if Einstein was dismissed, this theory would ultimately have re-emerged through the work of others. Although, this might carry some truth, history still shows that the status of the person from whom the theory originate does matter. To give another example, heliocentrism[14] was only taken seriously by Europeans after Copernicus had written about it in early 16th century, although the first account of heliocentrism dates back to Greek antiquity.[15]

---

13. Here is an article which recalls the beginnings of the theory of relativity from the point of view of the ether theory's proponents. Indeed, before the publication of Einstein's ideas and until the publication of the theory of general relativity in 1915, the notion of ether dominated the scientific circles: S. Goldberg (1970). In Defence of Ether: The British Response to Einstein's Special Theory of Relativity, 1905-191. *Hist. Stud. Nat. Sci.*, Vol. 2, pp. 89-125.

14. To have the sun at the centre of our planetary system, instead of the Earth.

15. Contrary to common belief, the transition between the two mathematical models was progressive: from the refutation of the Greek system to the exploration of alternative models. The progressive translation of the centre of the planet's trajectories from the Earth toward the sun is described in an interesting article that highlights the role of the astronomical school of Maragha during the thirteenth century: G. Saliba (1987). The Role of Maragha in the Development of Islamic Astronomy: A scientific revolution before the renaissance. *Rev. Synth.*, Vol. 108, pp. 361-373.

When Copernicus started teaching and writing about heliocentrism, he was already an established astronomer. It is then important to mention that the mathematical model proposed by Copernicus was no simpler than the geocentric one, that it was not better suited to the astronomical data available at the time, and that it did not allow for better astronomical predictions. Heliocentrism only provided a new sense of harmony.[16] But Copernicus already had a reputation, and his book was long awaited among the scientific community. And even if some rejected heliocentrism, like Tycho Brahe, the theory was still propagated through discussion within the scientific circles. This example shows that the origin of a theory, meaning the theoretician's persona and context, have a definite role to play in the theory's initial consideration.

b. *Relevance*

Once the origin of a theory is established, meaning that its source is trusted and deemed worthy of evaluation, it is the theory itself that is evaluated by the scientific community.

---

16. For an evaluation of the relevance of Copernicus' heliocentric model, see Kuhn, T. (1985). The Copernican revolution: Planetary astronomy in the development of western thought (Vol. 16). *Harvard University Press.* But as brilliant as Kuhn's account is, it unfortunately lacks the broader international and historical astronomical context in which Copernicus developed his model, i.e., the Muslim contribution. I thus recommend the following as complementary reading: G. Saliba, (2007). Islamic science and the making of the European Renaissance. *MIT Press.* The latter reading is valuable as it inserts Copernicus in a lineage of astronomical progresses.

Ultimately, it is the theory's relevance, or ability to explain and describe the world in which one lives that will determine its truthfulness. I specify "ultimately" because to propose a new theory is to propose new rules which are not yet part of science. Accordingly, there are no scientific recipe to develop new theories and the early stages of this endeavour often involve ideas and values that lie beyond the realm of science. Following the previous example, to choose between the geocentric model (Earth in the centre) and the heliocentric model (Sun in the centre), Johannes Kepler opted for the model that was most relevant to him. Because he was a fervent Neoplatonist, he was looking at the Sun as the physical manifestation of God. Accordingly, to put the Sun, or God, at the centre of the universe was for him an objective rather than a simple hypothesis.[17] To emphasize the role of value judgement in science, we can discuss Keppler's case further. Until Kepler, all motions were described in terms of lines and circles because these geometric elements were considered to be perfect, and hence, of Divine character. And this argument explains why the geocentric model proposed by Copernicus, a couple of generations earlier, was mathematically so complex and imprecise: because he was still using lines and circles to describes planetary orbits that actually are ellipses. By trading circles with ellipses, Kepler thus choose to make some Divine features prevail over others: to have the Sun-God at the centre of the universe was more important than

---

17. Ibid.

to preserve the Divine circles and lines. It is this shift in values that enabled him to make heliocentrism work. It is only after Keppler had described planetary orbits by means of ellipses (instead of compound circles and lines) that heliocentrism had noticeable scientific advantages over geocentrism. Only at that point was heliocentrism able to better explain astronomical observations and predict celestial trajectories with unprecedented accuracy. The superiority of heliocentrism was then described in terms of its precision and logic that was simpler and all-encompassing. I mean by 'encompassing' that the same logic was applicable to numerous other celestial bodies such as moons and galaxies. By 'simpler,' I mean that heliocentrism used a lesser number of independent variables when compared to geocentrism.[18] Heliocentrism then became more relevant in the sense that it solved some of the issues that were important at that time. Indeed, to be able to predict planetary trajectories enabled the development of better calendars, which in turn made society more effective and thus profitable. Note that I have translated 'relevant' in terms of scientific and economic advantages. By contrast, heliocentrism was not relevant to the Aristotelian conception of the universe, because it broke down the distinction between sub-lunar and super-lunar realms. Indeed, in a heliocentric model,

---

18. In order for the Ptolemaic geocentric model to remain consistent with the observations of planetary motion, it involved, for example, epicycles. These extra 'loops' were no longer needed in Kepler's heliocentric model, which was thus simpler.

the Earth is just a celestial body like any others. And this commonality implies that these other bodies are as corruptible as the Earth, which is in direct conflict with the Aristotelian's perfect and immutable super-lunar realm. But heliocentrism was relevant in scientific circles. The shift from geocentrism to heliocentrism thus exemplifies how theories are valued. This example shows that theories are judged via a combination of factors that range from simplicity to logic, to descriptive and predictive power. Broadly speaking, the more a theory becomes relevant, in the sense that it fulfils the contemporary needs of society, the closer to the Truth it will be deemed to be.

c. *Utility*

The value of a theory comes from its relevance, which is itself a combination of multiple factors: simplicity, logic and descriptive and predictive powers. But, in practice, as we have seen above, the overall acceptance of a theory will mostly depend on its usefulness. A theory can be considered to be true—to give a scientifically more accurate description of the world—without being recognized by the general public, or even by certain scientific communities. The value of a theory is judged in relation to the benefits (material, in our materialistic society) that it provides to the one who uses it. For example, in the scientific realm, the laws of hydrodynamics make it possible, for instance, to simulate the flow of water at the outlet of a tap. The interaction between water and the pipe could be done much more precisely by applying concepts of quantum mechanics, but from a practical point of view, 'classical' hydrodynamics is sufficient for the engineer. Similarly, the quantum theory is largely ignored by the general public because, although it is closer to the 'Truth', in the sense that it allows to describe more accurately the interactions between all the atoms constituting water, pipes, valves, and so on, this knowledge brings little benefit to the layperson. The two theories, classical mechanics and quantum mechanics, are therefore both considered to be valid, but in their own context. The first becomes a simplified version of the latter, but each retain its utility. Interestingly, by acknowledging that different theories can appropriately describe the same object but in different contexts, one is implicitly trading between precision and utility. I precision can be equated with truth, it means that one is living, at one's convenience, in different levels of truth. Accordingly, a theory like Newton's laws, even if known to be deficient, is still appreciated today because it serves the needs of a society that does not require a greater degree of precision. We, scientists, are thus dealing with different theories, different explanations, or different facets of the same truth, each being valid depending on what we are trying to study. One obvious example of differing theories used to describe the same object is the duality of light, which can be seen as either a wave or a particle depending on the phenomenon we are trying to explain. In short, when a choice must be made between multiple theories, it is the theory that is most useful that is retained. We have discussed previously the scientific relevance of a theory, and the utility discussed here is part of that relevance. By dedicating a section specifically to the utility of a theory, I wanted to emphasize that, in the final analysis, it is the practice of a theory that gives it its ultimate value. The more a theory is applicable in our daily lives, the more valued it will be.

d. *Section summary*

In summary, the acceptance of a theory passes first through an evaluation of its origin. In this aim, it is the person's credibility that will be key. Once confidence in the spokesperson is established, be it the theorist, the teacher or the journalist who conveys the message, the next step is to evaluate the theory's relevance to past and present observations: the better the description, while remaining scientifically logical and simple, the closer to the 'Truth' it will be deemed to be. But in the scientific realm, beyond the precision of a theory, or beyond its truthfulness, it is its usefulness that is given priority. Ideally both precision and usefulness should coincide. But in practice, it is the usefulness of a theory that gives it its ultimate value. To originate from a trustable source, to be scientifically relevant and, more specifically, to be useful, are thus the primary criteria that a theory needs to fulfil in order to be taken into account and validated. I will now turn to religion and discuss how the worldview promoted by Islam, which I like to call the "Islamic paradigm," fulfils these criteria.

2. Origin of the Islamic message

In my childhood, I never had to worry about Islam. To be honest, given the image of Islam that was portrayed by the media, I did not even want to know about it. It is only during my postgraduate studies, through students and friends, that I encountered a more appealing image of Islam. And it was only after apprehending the potential benefits of being Muslim that I began to explore this religion critically. Whatever the benefits, my first step was to check the origin of this religion. I thus started learning about the man behind the message of Islam: The Prophet Muhammad ﷺ. But when the person is no more, one can only refer to the legacy that he has left: the writings, the message preached, the description left by his family, friends and enemies. We are thus confronted with the notion of trust raised in the first chapter: How does one trust a man who died more than 1,400 years ago? For that purpose, I will proceed as stated in the second chapter: when faced with the impossibility of accessing directly the source (the Prophet ﷺ himself), I must evaluate it indirectly. This evaluation will thus be about the narrations and descriptions that have been reported. The goal is to build an image of his most probable character. Accordingly, the credibility of the spokesperson of Islam ﷺ will first be assessed through the evaluation of the historicity of the reported narrations, which will then serve as a basis for evaluating the character of the Prophet ﷺ.

a. *A historical account*

In this section, I discuss the historicity of the corpus which forms the textual basis of the religion. The corpus is comprised of both the Qur'an and *Ḥadīth*, which corresponds to all the sayings, actions and moments of life related to the Prophet ﷺ and his Companions. With respect to the Qur'an, from a historical point of view, its verses were written down during the lifetime of the Prophet ﷺ, although not yet compiled in one single book. The fact that the Qur'anic verses were immediately preserved in a written format ensured the initial preservation of the Qur'anic text. The parchments on which all the Qur'anic verses were written were then compiled in one single volume and duplicated in large numbers under the reign of Uthmān ﷺ, the third caliph and an early Companion of the Prophet ﷺ. This work of compilation and duplication ensured the perennity of the Qur'anic text. This explains why up to this day the Qur'an is considered authentic.[19] It should be noted that in those times, oral transmission was the norm. The transcription of the Qur'an was therefore an exception to the custom. I is through the remains of these exceptionally early transcriptions that we can, up to

---

19. Although I consider it important to refer to both followers and opponents of Islam, who may be both biased, I am only referring here to the book by M. M. Al Azami, a contemporary Muslim scholar who has been educated and served in the most notable academic institutions of the Western world: *The History of the Quranic Text, from Revelation to Compilation* (2003). See in particular Chapters 4 and 5, which relate the oral and written transmission of the Qur'an, respectively, as well as Chapter 6 which describes its compilation. And for those who are inclined to controversies, they will also find in Chapter 13 a sound rebuttal of the famous accusations made by A. Jeffrey in his *Materials For The History Of The Text Of The Quran; The Old Codices* (1937).

this day, appreciate the preservation of the Qur'an as an authentic historical manuscript.

By contrast, most of the Prophetic narrations were initially solely orally transmitted. It is only in the third century after the death of the Prophet 鐄, that an effort of compilation and classification has been made to safeguard these narratives in writing in order to protect them from possible forgery, falsification and errors of transmission.[20] Some figures involved in this effort of compilation, such as al-Bukhārī, Muslim, al-Tirmidhī, al-Nasā'ī, Abū Dāwūd, Ibn Mājah, Ibn Ḥibbān, Imām Aḥmad, etc., continue to be known to this day because they have literally dedicated their lives to the task. These individuals have, each in their own way, set up selection criteria to evaluate each transmitted narration. These criteria range from the simple verification that the various people involved in a chain of transmission have met (date of birth, death and place of residence, travel itineraries) up to the evaluation of the social status and character of the different narrators such as level of social recognition, potential material interest in reporting such and such teaching. Moreover, when the same narration is reported through multiple chains of transmission, it is then possible to crosscheck the different accounts and verify not only the authenticity of the different versions, but also their syntax. This work of comparison consequently enables the assessment of each reporter's memory and accuracy, which,

---

20. For an overview on the subject, I refer to the book of Mr. H. Kamali: *A Textbook of Hadīth Studies: Authenticity, Compilation, Classification and Criticism of Ḥadīth* (2005).

in turns, makes certain narrators prevail over others. As a result, this enterprise allowed for the classification of each narration on a probability scale. The highest categories of the classification (*Ṣaḥīḥ* = authentic and *ḥasan* = good) contain at the end a few thousand sayings and encounters. that are directly related to the Prophet 🕊 and his closest family members and Companions. It should be noted that this effort of compilation is unique in the sense that no historical event (prior to the digital age) has been documented with such dedication and precision. As a result, Muhammad 🕊, as a historical figure, is the only one among the founders of the other 'great religions' whose existence is historical undisputed. This work of preservation reached the point where we still have access, today, to the very own words of the Prophet 🕊, as they were uttered. Once the trust in the historicity of the reported accounts is admitted, one can begin to evaluate, through the reported words, the character of the Prophet 🕊. And it is the study of his life, based on what is closest to the truth, which establishes the trust that is necessary to evaluate the religious message itself.

b. *An honest, selfless and persistent man*

In this section I argue that, based on the reported narrations, the life of Muhammad 🕊 can only inspire admiration and trust. From a social point of view, Muhammad 🕊 was an established man: he was married and had a job. Before prophethood, he was already respected by all: although he was an orphan, he was of noble lineage and his foster carer, Abū Ṭālib, was a senior dignitary. He was recognized for his good conduct, moral character and sincerity: he was nicknamed (*al-amīn*). In terms of his environment, he lived with his tribe in arid lands. It is this apparent lack of natural resources and harsh climate that has protected this region from being under the domination of the imperial powers of that time. His prophecy started at the age of 40 and over the course of the following 23 years Muhammad ﷺ succeeded in rectifying deep-seated customs, through establishing a way of life and a religion that affected the economic and social order, locally and globally. Muhammad ﷺ literally changed the course of the world. He established the foundations of an empire which, in only few decades, overtook the superpowers of that time: mainly the Sasanian (Persian) Empire and the Byzantine (Roman) Empire.

During those 23 years, the Prophet ﷺ sacrificed everything in order to fulfil his mission: that of conveying the message of Islam. When the leaders of that time saw their power being threatened by the new worldview, they tried to silence the Prophet ﷺ by offering him women, wealth and power. He rejected this worldly bargain, and as a response he ended up being rejected by his own people. He remained faithful to his principles even in the most difficult moments of his life when he lost the most influential members of his family (i.e. his uncle Abū Ṭālib, who provided him with social protection, as well as his wife Khadījah, who was a source of emotional and economic support). The Prophet ﷺ spent all of his possessions for the cause of Islam. He suffered physical and psychological abuses, including systematic torture of his Companions, his rejection and subsequent pelting at Ta'if. His enemies tried to assassinate him and betrayed him in the most difficult moments, such as the assassination attempted on the day of his departure to Medina, the treachery of Jewish communities during the Battle of the Trenches. As soon as his situation finally improved in Medina, including the establishment of the intertribal peace treaty of al-Ḥudaybiyyah, the conquest of Mecca and subsequent recognition of his political authority by the surrounding tribes, the Prophet 🌸 opted for a life of extreme material simplicity[21] and forgave his bitter enemies for the sake of God, in hope for His reward.

In light of his behaviour, the hypothesis that the Prophet 🌸 went through a midlife crisis, that he was possessed, that he was suffering from some psychological disorders, or that he was thirsty for recognition and power, are unconvincing. Indeed, what would push a person to sacrifice his family, economic and social status and stability

---

21. I share here only one *ḥadīth* that illustrates the extreme altruism of the Prophet 🌸. The event is reported by his close Companion, 'Umar ibn al-Khaṭṭāb 🌸, and takes place while the Muslims were benefiting from an almost total control of the Arabian peninsula: 'Allah's Messenger 🌸 smiled while he was lying on a mat made of palm tree leaves with nothing between him and the mat. Underneath his head there was a leather pillow stuffed with palm fibers, and leaves of a saut tree were piled at his feet, and above his head hung a few water skins. On seeing the marks of the mat imprinted on his side, I ('Umar ibn al-Khaṭṭāb 🌸) wept. He said, "Why are you weeping?" I replied, "O Allah's Messenger! Caesar and Khosrau are leading the life while you are Allah's Messenger." He then replied. "Won't you be satisfied that they enjoy this world and we the Hereafter?"' *Ṣaḥīḥ al-Bukhārī*, Vol. 6, Book 60, *ḥadīth* 435.

to live a life of misery, materially speaking, and suffer the physical and psychological harms such as those en-dured by the Prophet 鬱? Even while in search of the truth before the prophetic mission including meditations and periods of prolonged retreat), there are no narrations which imply signs of madness or megalomania. On the contrary, the fact that he was trusted and loved by his contemporaries, friends and future enemies, illustrates an established psychological stability and integrity. It is indeed the altruism, devotion, constancy demonstrated by the Prophet 鬱 that inspire trust.[22]

c. *Section summary*

While the veracity of the Qur'an, as a historical manuscript, is established, the corpus of *Ḥadīth* is classified on a probability scale. Out of the hundreds of thousands of narrations that have been preserved, about ten thousand are ranked at the top of this probability scale. These narratives, by recounting everyday life's encounters, allows me to evaluate Muhammad 鬱, the man. They enable me to appreciate his motives and integrity. These narratives help me build trust in Muhammad 鬱. And it is only once trust is established that these narratives, along with the Qur'an, will serve as a basis to evaluate the message of Islam including its beliefs, perspective on life and practices.

---

22. I recommend the biography entitled *Muhammad: His Life Based on the Earliest Sources* by Martin Lings, because it is detailed while remaining fluid and accessible.

3. The material relevance of the Islamic texts

Once trust in the Messenger ﷺ is established, I can honestly evaluate, using scientific reasoning, the message carried by these narrations. As a modern scientist, I am particularly interested in evaluating the coherence of the texts (Qur'an and *Ḥadīth*) vis-à-vis contemporary scientific theories. This section therefore deals with the material relevance of Islam. The goal is not to use religious texts, and the Qur'an in particular, as a source of scientific facts,[23] but to appreciate the complementarity that exists between the scientific and religious worldviews. Regarding the material descriptions found in religious texts, I divide them into five categories:

    i. Recurring events. This category includes the description of common or known natural phenomena as well as the usual scenes of life.

   ii. Single events that took place prior to the Prophet Muhammad ﷺ. This category includes all the actions reported by Prophet Muhammad ﷺ which

---

23. I refer here to the scientific *I'jāz* movement, which desperately looks for so-called "scientific miracles" by linking modern scientific theories to specific scriptures. While I often agree with the interpretative reading of the religious texts in the light of modern scientific knowledge, I disagree with this movement's methodology and conclusions: the texts do not validate, in and of themselves, any specific scientific theory that was not known at the time. So far, I have never come across a scientifically explained phenomenon that unconditionally proves either the veracity of Islam or the existence of God. As a Muslim scientist, I do see miracles, but I maintain that they are subjective.

defy the apparent laws of nature. This grouping basically includes all the miracles associated with past Prophets.

iii. Single events that happened during the life of Prophet Muhammad ﷺ. This category includes all of his own miracles, as reported by his Companions.

iv. Prophecies that happened. This category includes all the prophecies made by the Prophet Muhammad ﷺ that did take place.

v. Prophecies to come. This category includes all the prophecies made by Prophet Muhammad ﷺ about upcoming events.

Note that I exclude here all descriptions of the invisible world such as jinn, angels, Day of Judgment, and Paradise, since they are not materially verifiable. And, for the purpose of this section, I define a 'miracle' as being any event that defies the apparent laws of nature and/or common logic.

After discussing a theistic vision of the physical world, I focus in a second part on the elements of category (i) that are to do with recurring events as they are mentioned in the Qur'an. The unique events of categories (ii), (iii), (iv) and (v) will then be treated together in a third part, since they all pertain to miracles. In a fourth section, I discuss what I call the all-encompassing nature of religion. Just like a scientific theory that acquires strength through its descriptive power, Islam also provides descriptions and guidelines that are relevant in each and every context of human life.

a. *Between natural phenomena and Divine will*

When trying to make sense of the world, one is often confronted with interpreting the different life's events either as pure physical and social phenomena, or as pure Divine interventions. My goal in this section is to show that this dichotomy has no justification. On the contrary, the religious texts suggest a dual vision of the world. According to the texts, the laws of Nature are to be seen as Divine expressions. From a historical perspective, with the industrial revolution and the advent of technology, many natural phenomena that were once solely described as emanating from Divine will, are now scientifically explained, and even controlled. For example, rain can be "seeded" in clouds with silver iodine. The American company *Weather Modification Inc.*,[24] for instance, has been offering such services since the 1960s. This artificial nucleation technique is used around major cities during winter time to prevent them from being blocked by excessive snowfall.[25] This method is also used during national celebrations and opening ceremonies to ensure beautiful sunny days.[26] Regarding agriculture, while people used to rely on God's

---

24. *http://www.weathermodification.com*

25. For example, see the following article https://www.reuters.com/article/us-russia-weather/in-russia-sometimes-it-rains-cement-idUSL1760049120080617 to see, at a glance, an unfortunate consequence of new technologies.

26. See the following article https://www.technologyreview.com/s/409794/weather-engineering-in-china/ for an overview of this technology as it was ten years ago.

favour for their harvests, today's hormonal treatments[27] and modern irrigation methods make it even possible to transform sterile lands into arable and productive ones.[28] Furthermore, using our knowledge of genetics, seeds can now be modified so that the plant produced is sterile (thus forcing the farmer to buy new seeds every year).[29] Appropriating through science what was exclusively attributed to God may suggest that science encroaches on the Divine by restricting God's realm of actions up to the point of replacing Him. It is indeed easy to assign to God everything that cannot be explained otherwise.[30] But why not seeing natural phenomena, physical laws and human actions themselves, as expressions of the Divine will?

---

27. The following is a technical article whose primary purpose is to show the current state of research concerning the control of germination by hormones: M. Miransari *et al.* (2014) Plant Hormones and Seed Germination. *Environ. Exp. Bot.*, Vol. 99, pp. 110-121.

28. Here is an example of a company that is specialized in the disruption of ecological environments to meet "market's needs": *http://desert group.ae*

29. Although this technology is prohibited for ethical reasons, patents exist and research continues. Here is an article that traces the development and describes how this technology works: L. Lombardo (2014). Genetic use Restriction Technologies: A Review. *Plant Biotechnol. J.*, Vol. 12, pp. 995-1005.

30. This conception of God refers to the concept of the 'God of the Gaps,' which is to ascribe to God all phenomena that humans do not understand. It is indeed tempting to use currently unexplained phenomena as a proof for God's existence. However, if one pursues this approach, the more one understands the world, the less Divine it becomes. And in scientific societies, where every phenomenon is expected to have a scientific explanation, there would be no room for God.

The Qur'an explicitly mentions that God acts through humans:

قُلْ هَلْ تَرَبَّصُونَ بِنَا إِلَّا إِحْدَى الْحُسْنَيَيْنِ وَنَحْنُ نَتَرَبَّصُ بِكُمْ أَن يُصِيبَكُمُ اللّهُ بِعَذَابٍ مِّنْ عِندِهِ أَوْ بِأَيْدِينَا فَتَرَبَّصُوا إِنَّا مَعَكُم مُّتَرَبِّصُونَ ۝

(التوبة ٩ : ٥٢)

Say, "Do you await for us except one of the two best things while we await for you that Allah will afflict you with punishment from Himself or at our hands? So wait; indeed we, along with you, are waiting." (al-Tawbah 9:52)

فَبَدَأَ بِأَوْعِيَتِهِمْ قَبْلَ وِعَاءِ أَخِيهِ ثُمَّ اسْتَخْرَجَهَا مِن وِعَاءِ أَخِيهِ كَذَٰلِكَ كِدْنَا لِيُوسُفَ مَا كَانَ لِيَأْخُذَ أَخَاهُ فِي دِينِ الْمَلِكِ إِلَّا أَن يَشَاءَ اللّهُ نَرْفَعُ دَرَجَٰتٍ مَّن نَّشَاءُ وَفَوْقَ كُلِّ ذِي عِلْمٍ عَلِيمٌ ۝

(يوسف ١٢ : ٧٦)

So he began [the search] with their bags before the bag of his brother; then he extracted it from the bag of his brother. Thus did We plan for Joseph. He could not have taken his brother within the religion of the

*king except that Allah willed. We raise in degrees
whom We will, but over every possessor of knowledge
is one [more] knowing. (Yūsuf 12:76)*

ٱلَّذِينَ أُخْرِجُوا۟ مِن دِيَـٰرِهِم بِغَيْرِ حَقٍّ إِلَّآ أَن يَقُولُوا۟ رَبُّنَا
ٱللَّهُ ۗ وَلَوْلَا دَفْعُ ٱللَّهِ ٱلنَّاسَ بَعْضَهُم بِبَعْضٍ لَّهُدِّمَتْ صَوَٰمِعُ
وَبِيَعٌ وَصَلَوَٰتٌ وَمَسَـٰجِدُ يُذْكَرُ فِيهَا ٱسْمُ ٱللَّهِ كَثِيرًا ۗ
وَلَيَنصُرَنَّ ٱللَّهُ مَن يَنصُرُهُۥٓ ۗ إِنَّ ٱللَّهَ لَقَوِىٌّ عَزِيزٌ ﴿

(الحج ٢٢: ٤٠)

*[They are] those who have been evicted from their
homes without right – only because they say, "Our
Lord is Allah." And were it not that Allah checks the
people, some by means of others, there would have
been demolished monasteries, churches, synagogues,
and mosques in which the name of Allah is much
mentioned. And Allah will surely support those who
support Him. Indeed, Allah is Powerful and Exalted
in Might. (al-Ḥajj 22:40)*

These verses illustrate how God's will is enacted
through humans. In other passages of the Qur'an, God even
takes ownership of human undertakings and endeavours.
God says, for example, that He created the ships and put
them at our service:

اللَّهُ ٱلَّذِى خَلَقَ ٱلسَّمَـٰوَٰتِ وَٱلْأَرْضَ وَأَنزَلَ مِنَ ٱلسَّمَآءِ مَآءً فَأَخْرَجَ بِهِۦ مِنَ ٱلثَّمَرَٰتِ رِزْقًا لَّكُمْ وَسَخَّرَ لَكُمُ ٱلْفُلْكَ لِتَجْرِىَ فِى ٱلْبَحْرِ بِأَمْرِهِۦ وَسَخَّرَ لَكُمُ ٱلْأَنْهَـٰرَ ۩

(ابراهيم ١٤ : ٣٢)

*It is Allah who created the heavens and the earth and
sent down rain from the sky and produced thereby
some fruits as provision for you and subjected for
you the ships to sail through the sea by His command
and subjected for you the rivers. (Ibrāhīm 14:32)*

وَخَلَقْنَا لَهُم مِّن مِّثْلِهِۦ مَا يَرْكَبُونَ ۩

(يس ٣٦ : ٤٢)

*And We created for them from the likes of it (ship)
that which they ride. (Yā' Sīn 36:42)*

وَٱلَّذِى خَلَقَ ٱلْأَزْوَٰجَ كُلَّهَا وَجَعَلَ لَكُم مِّنَ ٱلْفُلْكِ وَٱلْأَنْعَـٰمِ مَا تَرْكَبُونَ ۩ لِتَسْتَوُۥا۟ عَلَىٰ ظُهُورِهِۦ ثُمَّ تَذْكُرُوا۟ نِعْمَةَ رَبِّكُمْ إِذَا ٱسْتَوَيْتُمْ عَلَيْهِ وَتَقُولُوا۟ سُبْحَـٰنَ ٱلَّذِى سَخَّرَ لَنَا هَـٰذَا وَمَا كُنَّا لَهُۥ مُقْرِنِينَ ۩

(الزخرف ٤٣ : ١٢-١٣)

*And who created the species, all of them, and has
made for you of ships and animals those which you
mount; that you may settle yourselves upon their
backs and then remember the favour of your Lord
when you have settled upon them and say. "Exalted
is He who has subjected this to us, and we could not
have [otherwise] subdued it." (al-Zukhruf 43:12-13)*

Or, the contemporaries of the Prophet ﷺ already
knew that the design of a ship requires engineering and
qualified manpower to transform and assemble its parts.
Similarly, the ship's command requires a trained crew and
technicians capable of bearing the various damages. The
hand of men in this type of project is obvious, although
God designates Himself as the sole guarantor of its
creation and functioning. Similarly, when describing the
garden in *Sūrah al-Kahf*, God says that it is He who has
planted the vineyards, palms and other crops and set up a
river in the middle for irrigation:

۞ وَٱضْرِبْ لَهُم مَّثَلًا رَّجُلَيْنِ جَعَلْنَا لِأَحَدِهِمَا جَنَّتَيْنِ
مِنْ أَعْنَابٍ وَحَفَفْنَـٰهُمَا بِنَخْلٍ وَجَعَلْنَا بَيْنَهُمَا زَرْعًا ۞
كِلْتَا ٱلْجَنَّتَيْنِ ءَاتَتْ أُكُلَهَا وَلَمْ تَظْلِم مِّنْهُ شَيْـًٔا
وَفَجَّرْنَا خِلَـٰلَهُمَا نَهَرًا ۞

(الكهف ١٨ : ٣٢-٣٣)

62

And present to them an example of two men: We granted to one of them two gardens of grapevines, and We bordered them with palm trees and placed between them [fields of] crops. Each of the two gardens produced its fruit and did not fall short thereof in anything. And We caused to gush forth within them a river. (al-Kahf 18:32-33)

However, such an agricultural exploit, which was the pride of its owner to the point where the owner denied God's involvement in it, must have required constant maintenance. These examples show that the physical and divine explanations of a phenomenon simply correspond to the two sides of the same coin. To give you an anecdote, I remember during my stay at Swiss Federal Institute of Technology Lausanne (EPFL) that a colleague once marvelled in front of an optical phenomenon and exclaimed: 'Oh! This is God!'[31] I then naively retorted that it was only light. He was thus able to see God through a physical phenomenon while I was limited by the material. To see God all around me and within me is to realize that the Divine is expressed through each object and action.

---

31. Our objective that day was to align a spectroscopic system using three femtosecond-long pulses of light to generate a "photon echo." By adjusting the spatial and temporal alignment of the three pulses on a CCD camera, it was possible to visualize a double interference phenomenon: a grid of light formed by the superposition of vertical and horizontal interferences. By playing with the delay of one or the other pulse, one could modify this interference pattern. I admit that it was really cool but, at that time, I was unable to see beyond the material.

b. *Nature as described in the Qur'an*

Because I assume that ultimately both science and religion have the same source, which I see as God, I intuitively expect the Qur'anic descriptions of the physical world to coincide with scientific interpretations. In this section I thus go through some of the common Qur'anic references to natural phenomena and evaluate their relevance to modern scientific understanding. The is because the Qur'an does call for such scientific inquiry. Unlike the 'Enlighted' European civilization that has technologically prospered by opposing religion and science, Muslim civilization distinguished itself by marrying both. Indeed, the Qur'an, which served as the ideological reference for Islamic civilization, makes many calls to search for knowledge, use intellect, observe and pounder over the natural world:

وَمِنْ ءَايَـٰتِهِۦٓ أَنْ خَلَقَ لَكُم مِّنْ أَنفُسِكُمْ أَزْوَٰجًا لِّتَسْكُنُوٓا۟
إِلَيْهَا وَجَعَلَ بَيْنَكُم مَّوَدَّةً وَرَحْمَةً إِنَّ فِى ذَٰلِكَ لَأَيَـٰتٍ
لِّقَوْمٍ يَتَفَكَّرُونَ ۝ وَمِنْ ءَايَـٰتِهِۦ خَلْقُ ٱلسَّمَـٰوَٰتِ
وَٱلْأَرْضِ وَٱخْتِلَـٰفُ أَلْسِنَتِكُمْ وَأَلْوَٰنِكُمْ إِنَّ فِى ذَٰلِكَ
لَأَيَـٰتٍ لِّلْعَـٰلِمِينَ ۝ وَمِنْ ءَايَـٰتِهِۦ مَنَامُكُم بِٱلَّيْلِ
وَٱلنَّهَارِ وَٱبْتِغَآؤُكُم مِّن فَضْلِهِۦٓ إِنَّ فِى ذَٰلِكَ لَأَيَـٰتٍ لِّقَوْمٍ

يَسْمَعُونَ ۩ وَمِنْ ءَايَـٰتِهِۦ يُرِيكُمُ ٱلْبَرْقَ خَوْفًا وَطَمَعًا
وَيُنَزِّلُ مِنَ ٱلسَّمَاءِ مَاءً فَيُحْىِۦ بِهِ ٱلْأَرْضَ بَعْدَ مَوْتِهَآ إِنَّ
فِى ذَٰلِكَ لَأَيَـٰتٍ لِّقَوْمٍ يَعْقِلُونَ ۩

(الروم ٣٠: ٢١-٢٤)

*And of His signs is that He created for you from
yourselves mates that you may find tranquillity
in them; and He placed between you affection and
mercy. Indeed, in that are signs for a people who
give thought. And of His signs is the creation of the
heavens and the earth and the diversity of your
languages and your colours. Indeed, in that are signs
for those of knowledge. And of His signs is your sleep
by night and day and your seeking of His bounty.
Indeed, in that are signs for a people who listen. And
of His signs is [that] He shows you the lightning
[causing] fear and aspiration, and He sends down
rain from the sky by which He brings to life the earth
after its lifelessness. Indeed, in that are signs for a
people who use reason. (al-Rūm 30:21-24)*

أَمَّنْ هُوَ قَـٰنِتٌ ءَانَآءَ ٱلَّيْلِ سَاجِدًا وَقَآئِمًا يَحْذَرُ ٱلْأَخِرَةَ
وَيَرْجُوا۟ رَحْمَةَ رَبِّهِۦ قُلْ هَلْ يَسْتَوِى ٱلَّذِينَ يَعْلَمُونَ وَٱلَّذِينَ
لَا يَعْلَمُونَ إِنَّمَا يَتَذَكَّرُ أُو۟لُوا۟ ٱلْأَلْبَـٰبِ ۩

(الزمر ٣٩: ٩)

Is one who is devoutly obedient during periods of the night, prostrating and standing [in prayer], fearing the Hereafter and hoping for the mercy of his Lord, [like one who does not]? Say, "Are those who know equal to those who do not know?" Only they will remember [who are] people of understanding. (al-Zumar 39:9)

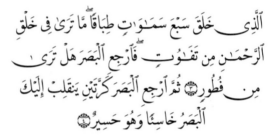

(الملك ٦٧ : ٣-٤)

[And] who created seven heavens in layers. You do not see in the creation of the Most Merciful any inconsistency. So return [your] vision [to the sky]; do you see any breaks? Then return [your] vision twice again. [Your] vision will return to you humbled while it is fatigued. (al-Mulk 67:3-4)

In these passages that God invites, and even challenges, mankind to engage in scientific pursuit (each at his own level), in order to learn about Him. However, it is important to remember that the primary purpose of the Qur'an is to guide mankind, that the Qur'an is a book of morality and salvation and not a scientific text. The Qur'an speaks primarily to the heart, and not only to the scientific mind. As a consequence, it must be borne in mind that the language of the Qur'an is often poetic and hyperbolic, which reflected the language of the Arabs in the sixth century.[32] Moreover, it should be noted that, by the intermediary of the Prophet Muhammad ﷺ, the Qur'an was initially addressed to an Arab population that lived far away from the intellectual centres of the neighbouring empires. One can understand that, in order to remain intelligible to the local tribes (who were scientifically unaware), the few scientific descriptions in the Qur'an are often figurative and personified, thus lending to multiple levels of interpretation. But the fact remains that the rare scientific articles mentioned more or less explicitly in the texts do fit with our current understanding of science.[33]

---

32. I admire the flowery language of the Qur'an and prophetic narrations. The consequence, however, is that, as a scientist, I cannot take the descriptions of natural phenomena literally (i.e. in their most evident meaning). For example, when it is mentioned that 'all were totally destroyed' (*al-Furqān* 25:39), the universal notion of the word *kull* (usually translated as "all") is restricted here to refer only to the peoples mentioned in the previous verse. Thus, the general expression is constrained by our contextual interpretation. Similarly, one may wonder whether the flood that occurred in Noah's ﷺ time affected the *whole* world; or whether his ark actually contained a couple of *all* the animal species existing in his time; or whether the enumeration of different types of livestock (*al-An'ām* 6: 143) is meant to be exhaustive, etc.

33. I retain only the Qur'anic descriptions of the natural world which are used to challenge the reader (for example, *al-Anbiyā'* 21:30: '... *will they not believe?*'), and which are only mentioned as evidence of the existence of God. I therefore exclude descriptions, such as

I will now go through some common examples and keep the details of my searches and thoughts in footnotes for the more curious:

THE CREATION OF THE UNIVERSE AND THE STANDARD MODEL

The Qur'an indicates that the heavens and the Earth have a common origin whose source is a smoke that expanded:

أَوَلَمْ يَرَ ٱلَّذِينَ كَفَرُوٓاْ أَنَّ ٱلسَّمَـٰوَٰتِ وَٱلْأَرْضَ كَانَتَا رَتْقًا فَفَتَقْنَـٰهُمَا ۖ وَجَعَلْنَا مِنَ ٱلْمَآءِ كُلَّ شَىْءٍ حَىٍّ ۖ أَفَلَا يُؤْمِنُونَ ۝

(الانبياء ٢١: ٣٠)

Have those who disbelieved not considered that the heavens and the earth were a joined entity, and We separated them and made from water every living thing? Then will they not believe? (al-Anbiyā' 21:30)

ثُمَّ ٱسْتَوَىٰٓ إِلَى ٱلسَّمَآءِ وَهِىَ دُخَانٌ فَقَالَ لَهَا وَلِلْأَرْضِ ٱئْتِيَا طَوْعًا أَوْ كَرْهًا قَالَتَآ أَتَيْنَا طَآئِعِينَ ۝

(فصلت ٤١: ١١)

{*Then He directed Himself to the heaven while it was smoke and said to it and to the earth, 'Come [into being], willingly or by compulsion.' They said, 'We have come willingly'. (Ḥā Mīm al-Sajdah 41:11)*

وَٱلسَّمَآءَ بَنَيْنَـٰهَا بِأَيْيْدٍ وَإِنَّا لَمُوسِعُونَ ۞

(الذاريات ٥١ : ٤٧)

And the heaven We constructed with strength, and indeed, We are [its] expander. (al-Dhāriyāt 51:47)

This series of events corresponds to the current Standard Model which suggests that the universe originated from a primary, dense and hot gas. After expansion and cooling, this soup of energy allowed the formation of the diverse particles that were then aggregated to give the current stars, including our sun and Earth.[34] It is also

---

the '*Sun setting in a muddy spring*' (*al-Kahf* 18:86), or the mention that '*God brings the Sun from the East*' (*al-Baqarah* 2:258), which describe the subjective perception of a specific person or people, Dhū'l Quarnayn and Abraham ﷺ, respectively), rather than a scientific statement meant to convince of the existence or the omnipotence of God.

34. For a detailed and accessible description of the Standard Model, its origins and consequences, see the book of S. Weinberg (1977) *The First Three Minutes*. The Qur'an, by its metaphorical language, can indeed be compared to the Standard Model. By the mention of 'smoke,' I understand that the Qur'an refers to a mass of hot particles. The accretion of this gas would have allowed the birth of stars and other heavenly bodies. Thus, this original nebula represents the common origin of the Earth and the heavens. I also acknowledge the mention of an expanding universe (*al-Dhāriyāt* 51:47). Once again, I appreciate the relevance of the texts with respect to the current conceptions of the world. With regard to the verses that mention the creation of the earth before that of the heavens (*al-Baqarah* 2:29 and *Ḥā Mīm al-Sajdah* 41:11); I suggest that the expression *thumma 'stawa ila'l-sama*" (sometimes translated as '*then He turned towards the "heavens*"') necessarily requires a metaphorical interpretation since, by creed, God is not constrained

specified that the creation of the heavens and the Earth was done in six days. The verse is then clarified with the statement that a 'day,' for God, can be equal to a thousand of our years:

اللَّهُ الَّذِى خَلَقَ السَّمَـٰوَٰتِ وَٱلْأَرْضَ وَمَا بَيْنَهُمَا فِى سِتَّةِ أَيَّامٍ ثُمَّ ٱسْتَوَىٰ عَلَى ٱلْعَرْشِ مَا لَكُـم مِّن دُونِهِ مِن وَلِىٍّ وَلَا شَفِيعٍ أَفَلَا تَتَذَكَّرُونَ ۞ يُدَبِّرُ ٱلْأَمْرَ مِنَ ٱلسَّمَآءِ إِلَى ٱلْأَرْضِ ثُمَّ يَعْرُجُ إِلَيْهِ فِى يَوْمٍ كَانَ مِقْدَارُهُۥٓ أَلْفَ سَنَةٍ مِّمَّا تَعُدُّونَ ۞

(السجدة ٣٢: ٤-٥)

It is Allah who created the heavens and the earth and whatever is between them in six days; then He established Himself above the Throne. You have not besides Him any protector or any intercessor; so will

---

by the space or time, which are themselves elements of His creation. Consequently, the conjunction *thumma* does not necessarily indicate a chronological sequence (in agreement with Hans-Wehr's possible translation of the word). Similarly, for God who is not constrained by this three-dimensional material world, the verb *istawa* cannot be taken literally as meaning "to climb on board," "to settle" or "to turn." The verse can thus be better translated as "moreover, He dealt with heaven." Note that other passages in the Qur'an mention the creation of the heavens before that of the Earth and what it contains (*al-Nāziʿāt* 79: 27-33). Consequently, the emphasis is put on the creative power of God rather than on the sequence of creation.

*you not be reminded? He arranges [each] matter
from the heaven to the earth; then it will ascend to
Him in a Day, the extent of which is a thousand
years of those which you count.* (al-Sajdah 32:4-5)

Another passage indicates that a "day," for God, equals
fifty thousand of our years:

$$ تَعْرُجُ ٱلْمَلَـٰٓئِكَةُ وَٱلرُّوحُ إِلَيْهِ فِى يَوْمٍ كَانَ مِقْدَارُهُۥ خَمْسِينَ أَلْفَ سَنَةٍ ۝ $$

(المعارج ٤:٧٠)

*The angels and the Spirit will ascend to Him during
a Day the extent of which is fifty thousand years.*
(al-Maʿārij 70:4)

These "days" can thus be referring to stages, with no
apparent restriction on their durations. These stages can
then refer to the epoque of the Big Bang theory, to the
eons, the geological eras, etc.[35]

---

35. It is interesting to see that the Qurʾan associates a number with the
age of the universe, while the contemporaries were not concerned
by such a datum. Both Greek and Zoroastrian mythologies, for
example, do propose a linear conception of time. Greek mythology
in particular refers to "Ages of the World" which are more
philosophical than material, with no details about their duration (see
Carlos Parada and Maicar Förlag, 1997: (http://www.maicar.com/
GML/%20AgesOfWorld.html). The book of Genesis also refers to the
creation of the universe in a succession of "days," up to the creation
of Adam ﷺ. After that point, the timeline is punctuated by the

CELESTIAL BODIES AND THEIR ORBITS

The description of the sun and the moon as sailing in the heavens, following a given path, is consistent with the notion of orbit. The sun revolves around the centre of the galaxy and the moon around the Earth:[36]

$$وَهُوَ ٱلَّذِى خَلَقَ ٱلَّيْلَ وَٱلنَّهَارَ وَٱلشَّمْسَ وَٱلْقَمَرَ كُلٌّ فِى فَلَكٍ يَسْبَحُونَ ۝$$

(الانبياء ٢١ : ٣٣)

---

genealogy of the different Prophets. The Qur'an follows similar timeline but emphasizes this notion of the relativity of time. The Qur'an thus explicitly calls for metaphorical readings that can therefore match with current scientific theories. With regards to the numbers themselves, the *Ḥadīth* corpus shows that the Prophet ﷺ and Companions were acquainted with large numbers (to count either money, goods or people, up to one hundred thousand). However, the texts often use conveniently rounded numbers to describe rewards and events of the afterlife such as a thousand (month or years) or seventy thousand (believers or angels). It is thus commonly accepted that the meaning of numbers, specifically in the context of rewards, unseen and afterlife, can goes beyond their numerical values to indicate something huge or uncountable. Similarly, the word myriad, while it corresponds specifically to the number ten thousand, is commonly used to indicate an indefinite number. With such understanding, the "days" mentioned in the context of the creation are not restricted to equate either one or fifty thousand of our years, but can refer to any lengthy period of time. And God knows best.

36. Although it must have been intuitive for Muhammad ﷺ and his contemporaries to explain that the sun and the moon revolved around the Earth following the wide-spread Ptolemaic geocentric

*And it is He who created the night and the day and
the sun and the moon; all [heavenly bodies] in an
orbit are swimming. (al-Anbiyā' 21:33)*

لَا ٱلشَّمْسُ يَنۢبَغِى لَهَآ أَن تُدۡرِكَ ٱلۡقَمَرَ وَلَا ٱلَّيۡلُ سَابِقُ
ٱلنَّهَارِ وَكُلٌّ فِى فَلَكٍ يَسۡبَحُونَ ۝

(يس ٣٦:٤٠)

*It is not allowable for the sun to reach the moon,
nor does the night overtake the day, but each, in an
orbit, is swimming. (Yā' Sīn 36:40)*

---

model, the fact that the centre of these orbits is not specified keeps
the text open to interpretation. Consequently, the text does also
match the current Copernican heliocentric interpretation since
both the sun and the moon are known to have their own orbit. I
would like to emphasize that the verb *yasbaḥūn*, which translates as
"swimming" or "sailing without full immersion" (translation from
Lane's Lexicon), implies, in its literal meaning, the stability of an
object that floats at the interface between water and air. If the
object in question is denser than water, it sinks; and if the object is
less dense than the air, it rises in the sky. Hence, in order to float,
its density must be between that of the water and that of the air.
Similarly, a stable orbit can only accept a body having a mass-speed
ratio of a certain range. Outside this range, the body will be either
driven towards the centre or ejected away from its orbit. I therefore
support the metaphorical interpretation of the word *yasbaḥūn*. From
the astrophysical point of view, I thus understand that *yasbaḥūn*
refers to a region of space that allows a stable orbit depending on
the characteristics of the celestial body. I appreciate, once again, the
relevance of the Qur'anic wording with current scientific notions.

THE UNIVERSE AND ITS FORCES

The description of the heavens as being maintained by invisible pillars and without abrupt boundaries corresponds to our conception of forces and their progressive field of action. In the case where the heavens refer to the extra-terrestrial space, these pillars then remind me of the gravitational forces:[37]

اَللَّهُ ٱلَّذِى رَفَعَ ٱلسَّمَـٰوَٰتِ بِغَيْرِ عَمَدٍ تَرَوْنَهَا ثُمَّ ٱسْتَوَىٰ عَلَى ٱلْعَرْشِ وَسَخَّرَ ٱلشَّمْسَ وَٱلْقَمَرَ كُلٌّ يَجْرِى لِأَجَلٍ مُّسَمًّى يُدَبِّرُ ٱلْأَمْرَ يُفَصِّلُ ٱلْآيَـٰتِ لَعَلَّكُم بِلِقَآءِ رَبِّكُمْ تُوقِنُونَ ۞

(الرعد ١٣ : ٢)

It is Allah who erected the heavens without pillars that you [can] see; then He established Himself above the Throne and made subject the sun and the moon, each running [its course] for a specified term. He arranges [each] matter; He details the signs that

---

37. Through the word "pillar," I understand a means to support and hold the sky, including all that it comprises, in place. Science today speaks in terms of forces, such as the gravitational force. Gravity, which on a cosmic scale prevails over the electromagnetic and nuclear forces, is effectively invisible to the human eye, and without apparent gaps or singularities between objects. Indeed, gravity follows a continuous and progressive function from one mass to another.

you may, of the meeting with your Lord, be certain.
(al-Ra'd 13:2)

ٱلَّذِى خَلَقَ سَبْعَ سَمَـٰوَٰتٍ طِبَاقًا مَّا تَرَىٰ فِى خَلْقِ ٱلرَّحْمَـٰنِ
مِن تَفَـٰوُتٍ فَٱرْجِعِ ٱلْبَصَرَ هَلْ تَرَىٰ مِن فُطُورٍ ۞

(الملك ٦٧ : ٣)

[And] who created seven heavens in layers. You do not see in the creation of the Most Merciful any inconsistency. So return [your] vision [to the sky]; do you see any breaks? (al-Mulk 67:3)

MOUNTAINS AND THEIR ROOTS

The description of the mountains as pegs, being anchored in the ground and standing up in the sky, corresponds to the fact that at the junction between two tectonic plates, while one is sinking, the other rises to form a mountain range. As a result, at this junction, the Earth's crust becomes thicker. The lower part of the crust forming a sort of root that supports the mountain above:[38]

---

38. The thickness of the lithosphere at the level of the mountains can reach 90km, which can potentially be referred as a "root" when compared to the oceanic lithospheres which are typically thinner (J. Jackson, 2004, Mountain Roots and the Survival of Cratons, *Astron, Geophys.*, Vol. 46, pp. 33-36). The Qur'an however states that it is these mountains that prevent the surface from "moving or shaking with us" (*al-Nahl* 16:15, *al-Anbiya'* 21:31). While the notion of stability in geology is debatable, it is interesting to note that indeed the upper part of the mountains corresponds to the edges of the continental

$$\text{وَٱلْجِبَالَ أَوْتَادًا ۞}$$

(النبأ ٧٨ : ٧)

And the mountains as stakes? (*al-Naba'* 78:7)

THE ORIGIN OF IRON

The description of iron as being "brought down" alludes to the fact that this metal is extra-terrestrial. We know today that iron cannot be produced in the hot body of the Earth, nor by the Sun, but that it comes from other stars:[39]

---

lithospheres, and not to those of the oceanic lithospheres. In other words, if the mountains were to move, our continents would move with them. More interestingly, it turns out that the oldest continental lithospheres, called cratons, also have "roots" that are more than 200 km deep. These cratonic roots partly explain the exceptional longevity of cratons, up to 3 trillion years old (MK Kaban *et al.*, 2015, Cratonic Root Beneath North America Shifted by Basal Drag from the Convecting Cantle, *Nature Geoscience.* 8, pp. 797-800). Alternatively, the subduction zone above which sits the mountain can also be seen as a "root." And depending on the numerical simulations, this submerged lithosphere can merge with these cratonic roots (A. Lenardic, 2003, Longevity and Stability of Cratonic Lithosphere: Insights from Numerical Simulations of Coupled Mantle Convection and Continental Tectonics, *Journal of Geophysical Research*, 108). If such is the case, the prolongation of the subducted lithosphere into the mantel, in other words, the mountain's "root", could potentially join the craton's root and participate in the longevity and to the so-called "stability" of the continental plates.

39. The fact that only a type Ia and II supernovae can produce iron (FX Timmes *et al.*, 1995, Galactic Chemical Evolution: Hydrogen Through Zinc *Astrophysical Journal Supplement*, 98, pp. 617-658) indicates that iron, along with the vast majority of elements, have been captured by accretion (BJ Wood *et al.*, 2006, *Nature*, 441, pp. 825-833). When the Qur'an says that God has "brought down the iron," I thus understand

لَقَدْ أَرْسَلْنَا رُسُلَنَا بِالْبَيِّنَٰتِ وَأَنزَلْنَا مَعَهُمُ ٱلْكِتَٰبَ
وَٱلْمِيزَانَ لِيَقُومَ ٱلنَّاسُ بِٱلْقِسْطِ ۖ وَأَنزَلْنَا ٱلْحَدِيدَ فِيهِ بَأْسٌ
شَدِيدٌ وَمَنَٰفِعُ لِلنَّاسِ وَلِيَعْلَمَ ٱللَّهُ مَن يَنصُرُهُۥ
وَرُسُلَهُۥ بِٱلْغَيْبِ ۚ إِنَّ ٱللَّهَ قَوِيٌّ عَزِيزٌ ۝

(الحديد ٥٧ : ٢٥)

*We have already sent Our messengers with clear
evidences and sent down with them the Scripture
and the balance that the people may maintain [their
affairs] in justice. And We sent down iron, wherein is
great military might and benefits for the people, and
so that Allah may make evident those who support
Him and His messengers unseen. Indeed, Allah is
Powerful and Exalted in Might. (al-Ḥadīd 57:25)*

---

that it can refer to the process of accretion. The Qur'anic expression
could also refer to the Egyptian understanding of iron as coming
from the sky, because of the Egyptian's exclusive use of meteoritic
iron (Comelli, D., 2016, The Meteoritic Origin of Tutankhamun's
Iron Dagger Blade. *Science*, 51, pp. 1-9). However, this last hypothesis
assumes that the Egyptian conception of iron survived the "Iron
Age" and the development of metallurgy techniques (~1000 BC), as
well as the 600 years of Roman domination of the nearby lands.
Indeed, under the Roman Empire, the best steel (a mixture of iron
and carbon) did not come from heaven, but from Indian mines (WH
Schoff, 1915, The Eastern Iron Trade of the Roman Empire *Journal of
the American Oriental Society*, 35, pp. 224-239). In any case, I marvel
once again at the relevance of the Qur'anic text to the past and
present conception of the origin of this metal.

THE ORIGIN OF WATER

Similarly, the description of water as coming from the sky or heavens also coincides with our understanding that, ultimately, water did come from space, as did all other elements.[40]

$$وَأَنزَلْنَا مِنَ ٱلسَّمَآءِ مَآءًۢ بِقَدَرٍ فَأَسْكَنَّـٰهُ فِى ٱلْأَرْضِ ۖ وَإِنَّا عَلَىٰ ذَهَابٍۭ بِهِۦ لَقَـٰدِرُونَ ۝$$

(المؤمنون ٢٣: ١٨)

And We have sent down rain from the sky in a measured amount and settled it in the earth. And indeed, We are able to take it away. (al-Mu'minūn 23:18)

---

40. Seeing that the water falls from the sky in the form of rain is obvious. But it is also true that ground water, such as the famous Zamzam spring around which Mecca developed, is as important and evident as rainwater. It is thus interesting that the Qur'an mentions explicitly that the water found on Earth originally comes from the sky. This passage can thus be taken at two different levels of interpretations. It could simply refer to rainwater infiltrating the ground, thus rendering it moist for plant to grow. Or it could refer, like in the case of iron, to the capture of water either during the accretion of our planet or transported by asteroids (AR Sarafian *et al.*, 2014, Early Accretion of Water in the Inner Solar System from Carbonaceous Chondrite-like Source, *Science*, 346, pp. 623-626). As a scientist, I thus appreciate the different levels of readings that the Qur'an permits; all of which are scientifically relevant.

WATER AS A SOURCE OF LIFE

Considering water as the source of all forms of life coincides with the current understanding of the origin of life and its development:[41]

أَوَلَمۡ يَرَ ٱلَّذِينَ كَفَرُوٓاْ أَنَّ ٱلسَّمَٰوَٰتِ وَٱلۡأَرۡضَ كَانَتَا رَتۡقٗا فَفَتَقۡنَٰهُمَاۖ وَجَعَلۡنَا مِنَ ٱلۡمَآءِ كُلَّ شَيۡءٍ حَيٍّۚ أَفَلَا يُؤۡمِنُونَ ۝

(الأنبياء ٢١: ٣٠)

Have those who disbelieved not considered that the heavens and the earth were a joined entity, and We

---

41. While it must be obvious for someone living in the desert to be aware of the importance of water and its necessity to both the animal and plant kingdom, modern science confirms it by adding a new level of understanding. Water apparently has unique properties that allow organic molecules to coalesce (Pollack *et al.*, 2009, Molecules, Water, and Radiant Energy: New Clues for the Origin of Life, *Journal of Molecular Science*, 10, pp. 1,419-29). I am referring specifically to section 2.6. Biological Coalescence, which deals with the evolutionist hypothesis of proto-cell formation. The coalescence of organic molecules means that organic molecules interact more with each other and that chemical reactions are enhanced. In addition, water is essential for the proper functioning of proteins and even play an active role in assisting their enzymatic activities (see Conti Nibali *et al.*, 2014, New Insights into the Role of Water in Biological Function: Studying Solvated Biomolecules Using Terahertz Absorption Spectroscopy in Conjunction with Molecular Dynamics Simulations, *Journal of American Chemical Society*, Vol. 136, pp. 12,800-7). Thus, even from an evolutionist point of view, water is not only essential to the formation of the original living being but also to the proper functioning and development of every living being. In other words, life, as we know it, would not be possible in any other liquids, and the Qur'an rightly points to this fact.

> *separated them and made from water every living*
> *thing? Then will they not believe?* (*al-Anbiyā'* 21:30)

THE EMBRYONIC DEVELOPMENT

The developmental stages of the human embryo described in the Qur'an correspond to our modern understanding of embryology:[42]

---

42. As for the embryological stages described in the Qur'an, I find it remarkable that the interpretative margin that is given allows these stages to agree with past and present observations. In particular, they agree with those of Galen (129-216 AC), famous for his medical research (*Corpus Medicorum Graecorum: Galeni de Semine*, translation by Phillip de Lacy, 1992, See the online edition of Berlin -Brandenburgischen Akademie der Wissenschaften). In his work, Galen describes human development in four stages (*Galeni de Semine*, section I: 8-9 pp. 93-94): (1) a seminal fluid, (2) an inarticulate piece of flesh that contains blood, heart, brain and liver, but without any clear distinctions, (3) a limbless silhouette including this time clearly differentiated heart, brain and liver, and finally (4) a being whose limbs are clearly differentiated. The Qur'an actually paraphrases these steps (*al-Mu'minūn* 23:14): (1) The first stage is called *nuṭfah* which translates to a "small amount of water" or "sperm" (translation from *Lisān al-'Arab*). It is also called *nuṭfatin amshājin* (*al-Jinn* 72:2), which translates as "mixed fluid" (*amshāj* translation from *Lane's Lexicon*). This first stage corresponds well to the seminal fluids that Galen mentions when he describes the meeting of the seminal fluid of man with that of the woman and their retention at the level of the uterus (*Galeni de Semine*, section I:7 p. 87). (2) The second stage is called *'alaqah*, and translates as "blood clot" or "leech" (translation from *Lisān al-'Arab*). At this stage, the embryo actually looks like a blood clot, from the blood it contains, its colour and lack of distinct form. But it also resembles a leech, through its parasitic lifestyle and potentially, its elongated shape. (3) The third stage is called *muḍghah*, and translates as "chewed piece of flesh" (translation from *Lane's Lexicon*). This imagery resembles the third stage described by

Galen by the fact that the embryo is only a trunk and posibly because mastication imprints would leave marks that resemble the somites of the embryo. (4) The fourth stage is described by the acquisition of bones and flesh, which implies the formation of the limbs and is therefore similar to the fourth stage described by Galen. It should be noted that the use of the conjunction "*fa*" between the different stages indicates a continuity in the development of the embryo, in agreement with our current understanding of embryology. Even if, in the light of the current sciences, these stages have been subdivided and renamed, the Qur'an's description remains valid. Hence, I appreciate, once again, the past and present relevance of the Qur'anic text. Contrarily to common belief, the Qur'an did not pioneer embryology, in the sense that the four stages described correspond to those described previously by Galen about 400 years prior to revelation. However, by comparing Galen's writings with the Qur'an, we note that the Qur'an does not include any of Galen's erroneous conclusions. For example, Galen erroneously acknowledges that the seminal fluid of the woman serves only as a nutrient for that of man, which contains all the reproductive essence (*Galeni de Semine*, section I: 7, p. 87). On this specific subject, the Qur'an is silent, and consequently remains neutral. Galen further states that sperm is the source of all membranous organs (veins, arteries, bones, nerve, etc.). He distinguishes these membranous organs from the flesh, which, he believes, originate from blood (*Galeni de Semine*, section I:11 p. 103). He also states that it is the most viscous substance of the sperm that will eventually give the bones (*Galeni de Semine*, section I: 9, p. 94). The Qur'an does not report any of these erroneous claims. Another example is that Galen takes as a source of seminal fluid (which he could have confused with the lymphatic fluid) the testicles, as well as all arteries and veins (*Galeni de Semine*, section I: 16 p. 136), while the Qur'an limits itself to the lower part of the abdomen (*al-Ṭāriq* 86:7), which includes the genitals of both man and woman. Galen also reports and contradicts other hypotheses concerning the origin of man that were circulating in his time. He criticizes for example some conceptions held by the authoritative Aristotle. Accordingly, Galen's views were just one among others popular conceptions. And it is therefore remarkable to see the Qur'an sorting out between popular beliefs and science by affirming only that which will later be confirmed by modern science.

ثُمَّ خَلَقْنَا ٱلنُّطْفَةَ عَلَقَةً فَخَلَقْنَا ٱلْعَلَقَةَ
مُضْغَةً فَخَلَقْنَا ٱلْمُضْغَةَ عِظَـٰمًا فَكَسَوْنَا ٱلْعِظَـٰمَ
لَحْمًا ثُمَّ أَنشَأْنَـٰهُ خَلْقًا ءَاخَرَ فَتَبَارَكَ ٱللَّهُ
أَحْسَنُ ٱلْخَـٰلِقِينَ ۞

(المؤمنون ٢٣ : ١٤)

*Then We made the sperm-drop into a clinging clot,
and We made the clot into a lump [of flesh], and
We made [from] the lump, bones, and We covered
the bones with flesh; then We developed him into
another creation. So blessed is Allah, the best of
creators. (al-Mu'minūn 23:14)*

Through these various examples, one can see that the
Qur'an does not come into direct conflict with the current
thinking in the physical sciences. Indeed, one can appreciate
that the Qur'an often coincides with our current scientific
knowledge even in the linguistic nuances of the words
used. I specify "often" because there are certain Qur'anic
descriptions that differ from modern conceptions, from
a philosophical rather than scientific point of view. For
example, the day and the night are described in the Qur'an
as two entities which penetrate one into the other, or wrap
around one another; whereas contemporary scientific
discourse refers to light and its absence:

ذَٰلِكَ بِأَنَّ ٱللَّهَ يُولِجُ ٱلَّيْلَ فِى ٱلنَّهَارِ وَيُولِجُ ٱلنَّهَارَ فِى ٱلَّيْلِ وَأَنَّ ٱللَّهَ سَمِيعٌ بَصِيرٌ ۞

(الحج ٢٢:٦١)

That is because Allah causes the night to enter the day and causes the day to enter the night and because Allah is Hearing and Seeing. (al-Ḥajj 22:61)

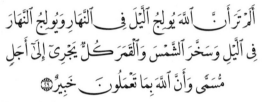

أَلَمْ تَرَ أَنَّ ٱللَّهَ يُولِجُ ٱلَّيْلَ فِى ٱلنَّهَارِ وَيُولِجُ ٱلنَّهَارَ فِى ٱلَّيْلِ وَسَخَّرَ ٱلشَّمْسَ وَٱلْقَمَرَ كُلٌّ يَجْرِى إِلَىٰٓ أَجَلٍ مُّسَمًّى وَأَنَّ ٱللَّهَ بِمَا تَعْمَلُونَ خَبِيرٌ ۞

(لقمان ٣١:٢٩)

Do you not see that Allah causes the night to enter the day and causes the day to enter the night and has subjected the sun and the moon, each running [its course] for a specified term, and that Allah, with whatever you do, is Acquainted? (Luqmān 31:29)

يُولِجُ ٱلَّيْلَ فِى ٱلنَّهَارِ وَيُولِجُ ٱلنَّهَارَ فِى ٱلَّيْلِ وَسَخَّرَ ٱلشَّمْسَ وَٱلْقَمَرَ كُلٌّ يَجْرِى لِأَجَلٍ مُّسَمًّى ذَٰلِكُمُ ٱللَّهُ رَبُّكُمْ لَهُ ٱلْمُلْكُ وَٱلَّذِينَ تَدْعُونَ مِن دُونِهِۦ مَا يَمْلِكُونَ مِن قِطْمِيرٍ ۞

(فاطر ٣٥:١٣)

He causes the night to enter the day, and He causes the day to enter the night and has subjected the sun and the moon – each running [its course] for a specified term. That is Allah, your Lord; to Him belongs sovereignty. And those whom you invoke other than Him do not possess [as much as] the membrane of a date seed. (Fāṭir 35:13)

خَلَقَ ٱلسَّمَـٰوَٰتِ وَٱلْأَرْضَ بِٱلْحَقِّ يُكَوِّرُ ٱلَّيْلَ عَلَى ٱلنَّهَارِ وَيُكَوِّرُ ٱلنَّهَارَ عَلَى ٱلَّيْلِ وَسَخَّرَ ٱلشَّمْسَ وَٱلْقَمَرَ كُلٌّ يَجْرِى لِأَجَلٍ مُّسَمًّى أَلَا هُوَ ٱلْعَزِيزُ ٱلْغَفَّـٰرُ ۝

(الزمر ٣٩:٥)

He created the heavens and earth in truth. He wraps the night over the day and wraps the day over the night and has subjected the sun and the moon, each running [its course] for a specified term. Unquestionably, He is the Exalted in Might, the Perpetual Forgiver. (al-Zumar 39:5)

Similarly, whenever the Qur'an makes broad descriptions, such as the age of the universe (*al-Sajdah* 32:4-5, see note 35, in III.3.b) or the description of the heavens as being maintained by invisible pillars (*al-Ra'd* 13:2, see note 37, in III.3.b), the text allows for an interpretive margin that makes it compatible with our current scientific knowledge. Indeed, the age of the universe is set at several thousand years, without any specification on the maximum number of years; and the invisible pillars can be interpreted as corresponding to the gravitational forces that govern the different celestial bodies in their orbits. It is therefore all the more interesting to read the Qur'anic text in the light of modern current sciences; not to prove that specific modern scientific discovery was in fact implicitly contained in certain verses, but to appreciate the current scientific relevance of a description of the world that dates back to more than 1400 years.

Regarding the theory of evolution, one should refer to the appendix for a detailed discussion. In brief, it must be kept in mind that, on the one hand, neither the Qur'an nor the Prophetic narrations clearly describe, from a mechanistic point of view, how living beings appeared on earth, and that, on the other hand, the theory of evolution is itself still evolving.

c. *Events that defy the scientific mind*

The Qur'an mentions multiples types of *āyāt*, or "signs" of God. For the "signs" that correspond to permanent natural elements, such as the sun, moon and other stars, as well as those that correspond to natural cycles, such as the alternation of day and night and the different cycle of life, they are all part of category (i), as mentioned above. Other "signs," however, refer to unique events that defy our current understanding of the physical world. Concerning category (ii) of past and unique events reported by Prophet Muhammad 鷺, I take the example of the staff of Moses 鷺 that turned into a serpent:

وَمَا تِلْكَ بِيَمِينِكَ يَـٰمُوسَىٰ ۝ قَالَ هِيَ عَصَايَ أَتَوَكَّؤُاْ
عَلَيْهَا وَأَهُشُّ بِهَا عَلَىٰ غَنَمِى وَلِيَ فِيهَا مَآرِبُ أُخْرَىٰ ۝
قَالَ أَلْقِهَا يَـٰمُوسَىٰ ۝ فَأَلْقَىٰهَا فَإِذَا هِيَ حَيَّةٌ تَسْعَىٰ ۝ قَالَ
خُذْهَا وَلَا تَخَفْ سَنُعِيدُهَا سِيرَتَهَا ٱلْأُولَىٰ ۝

(طه ٢٠:١٧–٢١)

*And what is that in your right hand, O Moses?" He
said, "It is my staff; I lean upon it, and I bring down
leaves for my sheep and I have therein other uses."
[Allah] said, "Throw it down, O Moses." So he threw
it down, and thereupon it was a snake, moving
swiftly. [Allah] said, "Seize it and fear not; We will
return it to its former condition. (Ṭā' Hā' 20:17-21)*

The passage from the staff to the snake, from an
inanimate object to a living creature, does not describe
a general law but a one-off event. The acceptance of
this type of miracles, because they are reported by the
Prophet Muhammad ﷺ through the Qur'an and Ḥadīth,
necessitates a prior acceptance of Muhammad ﷺ as a
prophet of God. It is impossible to prove these types of
miraculous "signs" without using a circular argument.[43]

---

43. Argument which consists in supposing as a premise what the
argument wants to prove. For example: Muhammad ﷺ is a true
messenger because the Qur'an says so; and the Qur'an is indeed the
word of God because Muhammad ﷺ said so. Hence, to base the
truthfulness of one on the truthfulness of the other is a circular
argument because each clause refers to the other.

Moreover, these signs cannot serve as a basis for belief. I would even go as far as to say that their function is to give an idea of the power of God rather than to strengthen a pre-existing faith.

Concerning category (iii) of the miracles of Muhammad ﷺ himself, there are specific occurrences where, for example, a small amount of food was sufficient to feed a large number of individuals,[44] or events such as the splitting of the Moon.[45] Since these events are transmitted by the Companions in the form of reported narrations, they are to be evaluated in the same way other *ḥadīth*s are: their degree of veracity increases with the cross-correlation of a large number of transmitters and their credibility. Indeed, the witnesses of this type of miracles are often the closest Companions of the Prophet ﷺ himself and any doubts one might have about them will automatically cast doubt on the reported fact. Between collective lies and truth, it is up to each and every one of us to study the life of these Companions, and then situate each reported narration on a veracity scale.

---

44. A number of Prophetic narrations indicate that in the presence of the Prophet ﷺ a small amount of food and water was sufficient for a large number of individuals. For example: "[...] Abū Ṭalḥah ؓ says: O Umm Sulaym! The Messenger of God ﷺ has come with his Companions and we do not have [enough] food for them. [...] The Messenger of God ﷺ says: O Umm Sulaym! Bring what you have. [...] In short, everyone ate their fill, and they were seventy or eighty men." *Ṣaḥīḥ al-Bukhārī*, Vol. 4, Book 56, *ḥadīth* 778.

45. For example: "[...] Anas reported: The inhabitants of Mecca asked him (the Prophet ﷺ) for a sign. He then showed them the splitting of the moon." *Ṣaḥīḥ al-Bukhārī*, Vol. 6, Book 60, *ḥadīth* 390.

If the events included in categories (ii) and (iii) are accepted as having occurred, they can be explained in three different manners. The first explanation is that they belong to events that follow the usual laws of nature, but have a very low probability of occurrence. The assumption is that they can be fully explained on the basis of our current knowledge. The second explanation is that they correspond to a natural phenomenon that are simply not yet understood. The hope in this case is that they will be explained scientifically in the future. The third option is that they are associated to a Divine alteration of the usual physical laws and, hence, it is impossible to explain them scientifically. Interestingly, quite a few common phenomena exist whose existence is not questioned but which science has no explanation for. For example, when it comes to explain life, for example, the passage from an inert amalgamation of embryologic cells to a living being, we currently have no consensus regarding when the embryo becomes "alive." Is it at the time of fertilisation, when the heart first beats? Or is it when the brain starts functioning? This confusion stems from the fact that there is no unanimous scientific definition of life. Similarly, the functioning of the brain can be well described by means of neurons, synapses, action potentials and neurotransmitters but, from these elementary electrochemical reactions, we are unable to explain consciousness. In other words, even if science is unable to fully explain these states of being, we are still confident that they exist. Consequently, the fact that science cannot explain the miracles of category (ii) and (iii) is not a reason to dismiss them outright, scientifically speaking.

Whether I can explain these "signs" or not, or not yet, becomes irrelevant if their role is to make us marvel. Indeed, as a scientist I do marvel at natural phenomena even if they are scientifically well established. As a believer, the "sign" fulfils its function in the sense that it points towards God and strengthens my faith. On the other hand, God says in the Qur'an that a sealed heart cannot believe no matter what miracle it might witness. Thus, he who refuses to see any Divine intervention can still see in these "signs" exceptional materiality. In either case, these unique events fulfil the function of bewildering their witnesses. The material and spiritual interpretations of these signs depends on the chosen theist or atheist framework.

Regarding category (iv), which comprises the prophesies of the Prophet Muhammad ﷺ, once again, we come to believe in the fulfilled prophesies through the trust we put in those who witness the scene and the chain of narrators. Let me mention for example the prophesied conquest of the Persian and Roman Empires,[46] or the prophesied preservation of Pharaoh's body.[47] These events correspond to

---

46. For example: "Abū Hurayrah ﷺ reported that the Messenger of God ﷺ said: The *Kisrā* (King of Persia) will certainly die and there will be no other *Kisrā* after him. And when the Caesar (King of Rome) perishes, there will be no Caesar after him. By the one in whose hands is my soul, you [Abū Hurayrah] will spend their wealth in the way of God." *Ṣaḥīḥ Muslim*, Book 41, *ḥadīth* 6973. This prophesy is all the more impressive because it was made while the Muslims were on the verge of being exterminated during the attack on Medina by the Meccans and their allies.

47. The pursuit of Moses ﷺ and his people by Pharaoh and his army, as well as their subsequent death in the Red Sea, was already recorded

situations in accordance with a common logic, in the sense that each of the predicted events is scientifically explainable and has a non-negligible probability of realization. As prophesies are not currently explained scientifically, the lower the probability of their realization, at the moment when they were formulated, the more these prophesies entwine themselves with a supernatural or Divine aura. Compared to the miracles of category (iii), these prophesies were known to a large number of people, including the enemies

---

in the Old Testament (Exodus 14:21-30 and 15:19-21). I therefore assume that this story was part of the Jewish and Christian folklore at the time of Muhammad ﷺ. The Qur'an rehearses the story even if it had lost its historical value. Indeed, in the fourth century AD the Christianisation of Egypt marked the extinction of the ancient Egyptian languages (including the hieroglyphs) that were already confined to the religious elite since the conquest of the nascent Greek empire in the third century BC. Consequently, all original accounts of these stories were either lost or unintelligible at the time of Muhammed ﷺ. Note that to this day, we have not found any historical records of these stories besides the Old Testament, which also means that the Pharaoh's identity is still debated. Indeed, neither the Qur'an nor the Old Testament specify the name of the Pharaohs in question. We know that the story of Moses ﷺ spans over two different Pharaonic reigns. Following historical accounts (of political instability and natural disasters), the story of Moses ﷺ could have taken place either under the reign of Ramses II and his son Merenptah, or under that of Tutmes II and his son Tutmes III, or under that of Amenophis II and Queen Hatshepsut. In conclusion, irrespective of the Pharaonic duo, the Qur'an rightly states that the body of this pharaoh would be preserved to serve as an example for future generations (*Yūnus* 10:92). Given the absence of sound historical records and the lack of knowledge concerning the preservation of the still buried bodies of the Pharaohs at the time of revelation, this statement was audacious.

of Prophet Muhammad 🕌 who would not have missed an opportunity to attack and ridicule him. Consequently, these prophesies have a stronger historicity because they were falsifiable and subjected to scrutiny. I thus suggest that they can be used to strengthen one's faith. However, the fact that prophesies are currently not scientifically explained does not necessarily imply that they are proof of the existence of God and of prophethood. But if someone is looking for proofs, since most scientific circles reject the truth of prophesies, I consider these prophesies to be the most convincing of the miracles because they defy modern science while having a solid historical ground.[48]

---

48. I am always cautious when looking for scientific miracles either to convince myself or others, simply because I fear that, if my faith is based on a specific scientifically unexplained phenomenon, it would then collapse if that phenomenon is later explained scientifically. For example, I always marveled at the fact that we always see the same face of the moon, and I initially thought that there was no physical reason why it should be so. Consequently, I used to consider this phenomenon as a hint that God exist... until I learned that it is a well-known phenomenon called "tidal locking" and that it is even quite common in our own solar systems. Does the scientific explanation make this phenomenon less miraculous? It would lose its status of miracle only if I was ascribing to God all the phenomena that I don't understand (see God of the gaps, note 30, section III.3.a). It would however retain its status of miracle if I define a miracle as something that generates awe, regardless of its scientific understanding. Similarly, Muhammad's 🕌 prophesies are so far considered scientific mysteries, but nothing guarantees that they will remain as such in the future. Hence, I would be cautious to base my faith on the prophesies' current inexplicability. But I do hold that, given their rare occurrence in common people, their abundance in Muhammad 🕌 makes him special, if not unique and can, thus, be indicative of his truthfulness.

In the category (v) which comprises the prophesies of the Prophet Muhammad ﷺ which are yet to be realized, or whose realization is subject to interpretation, I include for example the various signs of the arrival the Antichrist, the *Dajjāl*,[49] and that of the end of times.[50] Because the veracity of these prophesies is still to be proven or because their realisation is subject to interpretation, these events have value only for the believer.

---

49. I suggest here a narration that gives a rather detailed (figurative?) description of the attributes of the Antichrist and his actions: "al-Nawwās Ibn Sam'ān al-Kilabī ﷺ says: The Messenger of God ﷺ mentioned the *Dajjāl*. [...] He will be a young man with curly hair and a protruding eye; [...] He will come out of *Khallah*, between *Shām* and Iraq, and sow discord left and right [...]. He [will move] as fast as a cloud pushed by the winds [...]. He will ask the sky to rain, and it will rain, and ask the earth to grow its plants and they will grow ... [those who reject him] will suffer drought and be left without anything. [...]." *Sunan Ibn Majah*, Vol. 5, Book 36, *ḥadīth* 4075.

50. I refer here to Sheikh Imran Nazar Hosein, certainly the most prolific contemporary specialist in Islamic eschatology who, even if his interpretations are sometimes controversial, has the merit of daring to provide a contextual reading of the texts. For example, here is a narration that describes some signs of the end of time: "'Abdullāh Ibn 'Umar ﷺ says: 'Umar Ibn al-Khaṭṭāb ﷺ told me: One day while we were with the Messenger of God ﷺ, a man appeared, dressed in sparkling white with deep black hair. [...] He (the man) asked: Speak to me of the signs [of the Last Day]. He (the Prophet ﷺ) replied: [...] [it will happen] when the barefooted, poorly dressed, miserly, sheep guardians, will compete in the construction of high houses [...]." *Sunan al-Nasā'ī*, Vol. 6, Book 47, *ḥadīth* 4993. Following current interpretations, the shepherds mentioned in this narration correspond to the nomads who once inhabited the Arab States of the Gulf. The descendants of these people are today caught up in a mad race to build the tallest buildings in the world. The full narration is otherwise important because it defines the religion, belief, and spiritual purpose of the believer.

d. *An encompassing worldview*

In this section I argue that Islam is all encompassing in the sense that it is one of the few religions (if not the only one) which, not only provides answers to existential questions but also explicit and concise guidelines on how to benefit from every aspect of life. Indeed, Islam goes so far as to advise how to constructively interact with communities who uphold conflicting ideologies. In relation to science, Islam reminds me of the current theories of quantum mechanics and relativity, which are better approximations and are applicable in a wider context when compared to the previous laws of Newton, thermodynamics, electricity, etc. These modern theories are more encompassing because they have a greater descriptive power. They don't erase or ignore past conceptions but reaffirm apparent truth and simply correct or refine specific notions.

For example, quantum mechanics becomes most re-levant when the object in consideration is small (for example a molecule, atom or particle), and its energy is therefore "quantized"—the object is constrained to be or behave in specific ways. This quantization however vanishes when the system considered becomes larger. For example, a large system such as a battery delivers current, which is measured in amperes. At our human scale, the current follows the basic laws of electricity (Ohm's, Watt's, Kirchhoff's, among others). This current does, however, correspond to a flow of electrons, which are quantized and, when taken individually, do not follow any of these laws. We, however, are oblivious of this quantization of the current because our usual amp-metres are unable to resolve the electric charge of individual electrons. Similarly, relativity is relevant for objects that travel at speeds close to the speed of light. At such speeds, time and space behave differently than in our usual context: time is said to dilate and dimensions appear to shrink in the direction of motion. When these objects slow down, these effects become negligible, and the relativist equations approximate back to the usual kinematics equations. In other words, the "old" theories are not wrong *per se*, but simply not applicable in all contexts. Quantum mechanics and relativity are thus more encompassing because they include both the general as well as the specific contexts.[51]

Similarly, the strength of Islam also resides in its ability to explain human origin and destination, as well as the origins and divergences of other religions. Islam neither erases nor dismisses other faiths but recognizes them and simply corrects and refines what notions of faith ought to be. As a Muslim, I believe that all other faiths have a Divine origin, but that due to diverse political, economic and social pressures, their original message and practice have been understandably distorted. That is why I never considered my conversion as reboot of my Catholic Christian firmware but more as a software update that preserved the same basic belief in God. It refined the description of Jesus while it

---

51. In theory, we should be able to use quantum mechanics and general relativity to calculate with ultra-high precision how much energy is required to cook an egg, or when a train will reach its destination. These methods are however extremely demanding in terms of computational power, and are not worth the bother given the fact that, at our scale, we do not require such precision.

preserved the same overall morals and asked for coherent practices. The fact that other faiths are given some validity, while the differences are clearly stated, is key to engage in constructive discussions and societal engagement. Indeed, the Qur'an and *Ḥadīth* give clear guidance on how to deal with other faiths, whether they are spiritualist, theist or materialist; whether these communities are majorities under whom Muslims live or minorities under Muslim rule.[52] For example, in the extreme and most precarious cases when the worldviews diametrically oppose each other resulting in enmity, Islam still requires good conduct (for example *Ṭā' Hā'* 20:44, when Moise is asked to politely invite Pharaoh to believe), respect of contractual agreements (for example *al-Tawbah* 9:4), and the granting of protection and assistance whenever it is sought (for example *al-Tawbah* 9:6). Islam is all encompassing because it is a source of advice and inspiration for all spheres of live: including private, familial, social, economic, political. It reminds me of Einstein's quest to find a unifying theory that describes all the applying forces in the universe.[53] Similarly, Islam is my "grand unified

---

52. I would like to emphasize that the theoretical framework on how to deal with non-Muslim communities is set by the Prophet 🕌. It is not to be extracted from historical accounts of the following generations of Muslim rulers, which, at best, only represent a contextual understanding and a contextual application of this ideal. Because the application might differ from the theory, it is important to differentiate between the two.

53. This quest for developing a unifying theory started in fact with James Maxwell in the mid 1800's when he derived his famous equations that unified, for the first time, electricity and magnetism. Since then, the universe was believed to be dictated by four fundamental forces: electromagnetism, gravity, weak interaction and strong

theory" because it solves all existential questions and provides a practical and constructive approach on how to behave in all contexts. Islam even helps me consider and deal with people whose conception of the world is different than mine, and as such is it all encompassing.

e. *Section summary*

In summary, I showed that the two visions, the scientific and the religious, do not oppose each other. On the contrary, I see both as two faces of the same coin. As for the few physical descriptions found in the sacred texts, I appreciate their past and present scientific relevance. Especially with regard to the Qur'an, considered as the ultimate miracle, it is its literary accuracy, coherence and applicability that give it its miraculous character. By miraculous I mean something that exceeds all expectations of a human being having lived 1400 years ago in a scientifically neglected corner of the Arabian Peninsula. I also argue that realized prophesies can also help strengthen belief. I however insist that my goal is not to look for particular miracles on which I could base my faith, but to show that to believe, from an Islamic point of view, is a scientifically sound choice. Indeed, when the

---

interaction. Einstein pursued this quest by developing his general relativity,which unified gravitation with Maxwell's electromagnetism in the early 1900. The electroweak interaction was added to the group in the late 1900's, giving rise to photons and bosons. Current efforts are nowadays made to include the strong interactions to give a grand unified theory, namely a "theory of everything," which would englobe general relativity and quantum mechanics.

texts refer to some natural phenomena for which science has an explanation, I appreciate that both descriptions are in accordance with each other. I further described this religion as being all encompassing in the sense that it gives meaning to this world, and that it positively influences all aspects of my life. While I haved devoted part of this section to reading the revealed texts with scientific lenses, I would like to remind the reader that Islam gives much more than a description of the material world. Indeed, beyond the material, the primary purpose of this religion is to teach about God and inform about the unseen world. In this aim, the "signs," or miracles, are used as persuasive arguments; they point toward God and reinforce an already established faith, but are not, in and of themselves, indisputable arguments for the existence of God. In other words, if one does not want to see these signs as evidences for God, he can certainly do so, as did the Pharaoh while witnessing some of God's "greatest signs" (*Ṭā' Hā'* 20:23). I must also note that the impossibility of a scientific explanation of certain events is not sufficient as an argument to dismiss a religion or the existance of God. Indeed, to confront events that do not fit our current scientific understanding of the world is quite common in science and it is what motivates us, scientists, to pursue our work. When it comes to the sciptures, when confronting unexplained events, we should always start by evaluating the historicity of the report and its metaphorical interpretation. And if their account still contradict our current understanding of the natural world, then it is up to each individual to interpret these unexplained events either as natural phenomena that are yet to be explained, or as a direct Divine intervention. As long as the unexplaind events remain that way, the chosen interpretation will simply reflect a preconcieved belief about the world. But neither interpretation is antagonist to faith. Indeed, the believer can either expect God to act directly by violating the natural order, or indirectly through the laws of nature. Hence, to be unable to explain certain events is not detrimental to faith in either science or God. I will end by stating that, while I can understand both, the atheist and theist views of the world, given my current scientific understanding of the world and of this religion, to believe in a Divine orchestration of the world is simply more convincing than to believe that this world is the result of a fortuitus sequence of random events or mere quantum fluctuations.

4. Internal logic of the Islamic paradigm

In order to continue my scientific evaluation of Islam, I now turn to what I call its internal logic. By "internal logic" I refer to the notions of, for example, freewill, goodness, and success that Islam defines in order to help us comprehend this world. It is important to define these notions because they frame the way we conceptualize this world as well as our objectives and the ways we undertake to reach these objectives. Furthermore, to provide explicit definitions is important because framing these notions can readily be altered by social customs. Islam thus corrects these notions the same way that modern scientific theories correct outdated conceptions of the world. Indeed, to fully benefit from quantum and relativistic theory, as a scientist, I must revisit my intuitive notions of space and time. On one hand, quantum theory assumes that, although usual objects have specific sizes and positions, the particles they are made from do not obey the same rules. Electrons, for example, cannot be defined by their size and position but by their probability of presence. On the other hand, general relativity predicts, for example, that time passes differently for people moving at different speeds. Accordingly, to fully benefit from these theories, we are asked to correct notions in ways that are counter intuitive. Similarly, if I want to fully benefit from Islam, I also need to revisit certain notions. To illustrate the underlying logic of Islam, I will discuss in this section the notions of freewill, of determinism, of good and evil, and of success and failure. Understandably, to do so appropriately, I will presuppose the existence of God and the veracity of the sacred texts.

a. *Notions of freewill and determinism*

In this section, I will discuss my conception of conditional freewill, which stands as a middle ground between pure determinism and absolute freedom. In order to better comprehend these terms, I will refer once more to scientific notions. Current science assumes that the world is causal, meaning that specific actions have specific consequences, and that every time the same cause takes place, the same consequence will also take place. The objective of scientific theories is thus to define these causal relations, often by means of equations. In some ways, these equations not only allow one to understand the past and the present but, more importantly, they allow one to predict future events. Let's now imagine that we can fully describe this material universe with equations. In other words, let's imagine that every single event is the logical consequence of well-defined causes. Each cause in turn is also the result of previous causes, and so on and so forth until the very first instant of this universe. I then come to the conclusion that whoever knows about this first instant is necessarily aware of its governing laws and the states of each of its constituents at any point in time, be it past, present or future. If I accept that God is at the origin of this universe, and if I accept that this universe is causal, then it becomes evident that every object, as well as every event, in this universe, no matter how small or big, falls under His knowledge, like the result of a mathematical equation. Such a world would thus be fully deterministic, in the sense that our choices would solely be a product of our material being and environment. In such a world, freewill would be a mere illusion. This type of determinism is indeed implied, for example, through the premonitory dreams of Joseph ﷺ when he sees his family bowing down to him:

إِذْ قَالَ يُوسُفُ لِأَبِيهِ يَـٰٓأَبَتِ إِنِّى رَأَيْتُ أَحَدَ عَشَرَ كَوْكَبًا وَٱلشَّمْسَ وَٱلْقَمَرَ رَأَيْتُهُمْ لِى سَـٰجِدِينَ ۝

(يوسف ١٢:٤)

[Of these stories mention] when Joseph said to his father, "O my father, indeed I have seen [in a dream]

eleven stars and the sun and the moon; I saw them
prostrating to me." (*Yūsuf* 12:4)

وَرَفَعَ أَبَوَيْهِ عَلَى ٱلْعَرْشِ وَخَرُّوا۟ لَهُۥ سُجَّدًا ۖ وَقَالَ يَـٰٓأَبَتِ
هَـٰذَا تَأْوِيلُ رُءْيَـٰىَ مِن قَبْلُ قَدْ جَعَلَهَا رَبِّى حَقًّا ۖ وَقَدْ أَحْسَنَ
بِىٓ إِذْ أَخْرَجَنِى مِنَ ٱلسِّجْنِ وَجَآءَ بِكُم مِّنَ ٱلْبَدْوِ مِنۢ بَعْدِ
أَن نَّزَغَ ٱلشَّيْطَـٰنُ بَيْنِى وَبَيْنَ إِخْوَتِىٓ ۚ إِنَّ رَبِّى لَطِيفٌ
لِّمَا يَشَآءُ ۚ إِنَّهُۥ هُوَ ٱلْعَلِيمُ ٱلْحَكِيمُ ۝

(يوسف ١٢: ١٠٠)

*And he raised his parents upon the throne, and they
bowed to him in prostration. And he said, "O my
father, this is the explanation of my vision of before.
My Lord has made it reality. And He was certainly
good to me when He took me out of prison and brought
you [here] from Bedouin life after Satan had induced
[estrangement] between me and my brothers. Indeed,
my Lord is Subtle in what He wills. Indeed, it is He
who is the Knowing, the Wise." (Yūsuf 12:100)*

In this example, God had informed Joseph ﷺ,
by means of dreams, about his family's submission and
reverence decades before the actual event took place. And
the event took place without the use of any supernatural
events. The prophesy thus implies determinism. From
a scientific point of view, determinism in turn implies

that every object is governed by well-defined laws and forces. And by obeying these laws, each object has a well-defined objective. In thermodynamics, for example, one of these objectives will be the increase of entropy or the minimization of internal energy. The degree of achievement of these objectives will depend on the initial conditions and factors that may interact with the object.

To give an example, a raindrop is subject to Earth's gravitation. The drop will keep on falling and flowing until it reaches the lowest point possible. The objective of the drop is to fall. Surface tension, wind, soil type and temperature are some of the factors that influence the achievement of that objective. The surface tension will determine the geometry and size of the drop and, consequently, the speed at which it falls; the wind will change its trajectory; the soil type will dictate its flow once it hits the ground; the temperature will influence its viscosity and thus the ways it will flow through the ground, and so on. If we are able to take all these parameters into account, the degree of accomplishment of the drop's objective, in other words, its final position, could have been calculated as soon as it formed in the clouds. Like the raindrop, I also have an objective, which is to worship God. Indeed, God informs that the sole purpose of man is to worship Him.

وَمَا خَلَقْتُ ٱلْجِنَّ وَٱلْإِنسَ إِلَّا لِيَعْبُدُونِ ۝

(الذاريات ٥١:٥٦)

And I did not create the jinn and mankind except to worship Me. (al-Dhāriyāt 51:56)

Also like the rain drop, my objective is also influenced by multiple factors such as my desires, intellect, physical abilities, social context, and so on. All these factors will influence the extent to which I will fulfil my worship. With such a causal view of the world, all my future actions and choices could have been predicted based on my actual living conditions and experiences. However, God indicates that man differs from other creatures, such as angels, animals, plants and inanimate objects, in that he has opted for the "trust," which is commonly understood as referring to free-will:

$$إِنَّا عَرَضْنَا ٱلْأَمَانَةَ عَلَى ٱلسَّمَـٰوَٰتِ وَٱلْأَرْضِ وَٱلْجِبَالِ فَأَبَيْنَ أَن يَحْمِلْنَهَا وَأَشْفَقْنَ مِنْهَا وَحَمَلَهَا ٱلْإِنسَـٰنُ إِنَّهُۥ كَانَ ظَلُومًا جَهُولًا ۝$$

(الأحزاب ٣٣: ٧٢)

Indeed, we offered the trust to the heavens and the earth and the mountains, and they declined to bear it and feared it; but man [undertook to] bear it. Indeed, he was unjust and ignorant. (al-Aḥzāb 33:72)

God has thus given me the opportunity to voluntarily walk towards my objective, or to turn away from it. He has given me the opportunity to recognize Him through His signs, or to be heedless of Him; to submit to Him through each of my actions or to defy Him. To give another example, when I undertake a journey and reach an intersection, I have the choice to take any junction, regardless if it takes me closer to my destination or further away. This choice constitutes the freewill that is given to me. However, the different roads correspond to pre-established conditions which are under God's control. God has indeed declared Himself to be omnipotent:

هُوَ ٱللَّهُ ٱلَّذِى لَآ إِلَٰهَ إِلَّا هُوَ عَٰلِمُ ٱلْغَيْبِ وَٱلشَّهَٰدَةِ

هُوَ ٱلرَّحْمَٰنُ ٱلرَّحِيمُ ۞ هُوَ ٱللَّهُ ٱلَّذِى لَآ إِلَٰهَ إِلَّا هُوَ

ٱلْمَلِكُ ٱلْقُدُّوسُ ٱلسَّلَٰمُ ٱلْمُؤْمِنُ ٱلْمُهَيْمِنُ ٱلْعَزِيزُ ٱلْجَبَّارُ

ٱلْمُتَكَبِّرُ سُبْحَٰنَ ٱللَّهِ عَمَّا يُشْرِكُونَ ۞ هُوَ ٱللَّهُ ٱلْخَٰلِقُ

ٱلْبَارِئُ ٱلْمُصَوِّرُ لَهُ ٱلْأَسْمَآءُ ٱلْحُسْنَىٰ يُسَبِّحُ لَهُۥ مَا فِى

ٱلسَّمَٰوَٰتِ وَٱلْأَرْضِ وَهُوَ ٱلْعَزِيزُ ٱلْحَكِيمُ ۞

(الحشر ٥٩: ٢٢-٢٤)

He is Allah, other than whom there is no deity, Knower of the unseen and the witnessed. He is the Entirely Merciful, the Especially Merciful. He is Allah, other than whom there is no deity, the Sovereign, the Pure, the Perfection, the Bestower of Faith, the Overseer, the Exalted in Might, the Compeller, the Superior. Exalted is Allah above whatever they associate with Him. He is Allah, the Creator, the Inventor, the Fashioner;

to Him belong the best names. Whatever is in the heavens and earth is exalting Him. And He is the Exalted in Might, the Wise. (al-Ḥashr 59:22-24)

God can therefore add or subtract a road to the junction, without necessarily following the rules of common logic. God can indeed defy the natural order of events, as is the case with the resurrection of birds that Abraham 🕮 had cut off, or the unexpected pregnancy of Mary, mother of Jesus 🕮:

وَإِذْ قَالَ إِبْرَاهِـمُ رَبِّ أَرِنِى كَيْفَ تُحْىِ ٱلْمَوْتَىٰ قَالَ أَوَلَمْ
تُؤْمِن قَالَ بَلَىٰ وَلَـٰكِن لِّيَطْمَئِنَّ قَلْبِى قَالَ فَخُذْ أَرْبَعَةً مِّنَ
ٱلطَّيْرِ فَصُرْهُنَّ إِلَيْكَ ثُمَّ ٱجْعَلْ عَلَىٰ كُلِّ جَبَلٍ مِّنْهُنَّ جُزْءًا
ثُمَّ ٱدْعُهُنَّ يَأْتِينَكَ سَعْيًا وَٱعْلَمْ أَنَّ ٱللَّهَ عَزِيزٌ حَكِيمٌ ﴿﴾

(البقرة ٢: ٢٦٠)

And [mention] when Abraham said, "My Lord, show me how You give life to the dead." [Allah] said, "Have you not believed?" He said, "Yes, but [I ask] only that my heart may be satisfied." [Allah] said, "Take four birds and commit them to yourself. Then [after slaughtering them] put on each hill a portion of them; then call them – they will come [flying] to you in haste. And know that Allah is Exalted in Might and Wise." (al-Baqarah 2:260)

قَالَتْ رَبِّ أَنَّىٰ يَكُونُ لِى وَلَدٌ وَلَمْ يَمْسَسْنِى بَشَرٌ قَالَ كَذَٰلِكِ اللَّهُ يَخْلُقُ مَا يَشَآءُ إِذَا قَضَىٰٓ أَمْرًا فَإِنَّمَا يَقُولُ لَهُۥ كُن فَيَكُونُ ۝

(آل عمران ٣: ٤٧)

She said, "My Lord, how will I have a child when no man has touched me?" [The angel] said, "Such is Allah; He creates what He wills. When He decrees a matter, He only says to it, "Be," and it is." (Āl 'Imrān 3:47)

Note however that each time the apparent laws of nature were broken (as reported in the religious texts), it was either for Prophets or for common people who would then go on to carry the burden of prophethood by being living proofs of God,such as the people of the cave, the man and his donkey. As a commoner, I should not expect any such breaking of natural laws to happen in my favour (for example in *al-An'ām* 6:158) but I can still expect an unexpected sequence of circumstances that would have a similar effect to breaking the natural order of things.[54] Furthermore, depending on my behaviour, God keeps to Himself the prerogative of facilitating one route or another:

---

54. To give a specific example, one day in Geneva, I found myself to be particularly heedless of the religious precepts and simply tried to forget about them few days later, on the way to Vevey, I lost in the train my bag on the train, it contained quite a few valuable items: my wallet, a few thousands Swiss francs' worth of electronics, a hard drive containing the last few months of full processed, work-related data and a notebook containing about a decade of personal notes. At that time, I did not want to see any relationship between my possible

فَأَمَّا مَنْ أَعْطَىٰ وَٱتَّقَىٰ ۞ وَصَدَّقَ بِٱلْحُسْنَىٰ ۞
فَسَنُيَسِّرُهُ لِلْيُسْرَىٰ ۞ وَأَمَّا مَنْ بَخِلَ وَٱسْتَغْنَىٰ ۞
وَكَذَّبَ بِٱلْحُسْنَىٰ ۞ فَسَنُيَسِّرُهُ لِلْعُسْرَىٰ ۞

(الليل ٩٢: ٥-١٠)

As for he who gives and fears Allah, and believes in the best [reward], We will ease him toward ease. But as for he who withholds and considers himself free of need and denies the best [reward], We will ease him toward difficulty. (al-Layl 92:5-10)

God can also affect my perceptions so as to make me prefer a certain path, just as He had made the enemy troops appear small in the eyes of the first Muslims in order to give them hope and strength:

---

heedlessness and this loss. But a month later, when the lost-and-found office in Geneva contacted me and asked me to retrieve the remnants of my bag, and when the person at the counter told me, without having asked him, that it was found at the exact same place where I had potentially transgressed in Geneva, I could not see in this loss anything but a Divine punishment. To be Divinely reprimanded for a potential mistake might seem preposterous, but it was at a time when I felt spiritually high, and although I felt close to God, I became heedless to one of His commands. Of course, I can imagine to logical physical sequences of events to explain what happened to my bag. But the probability of finding the bag that I had lost on a train while leaving Geneva, when back in Geneva at that specific location, which is quite far away from the train station, is so low that it simply defies my expectations. May God forgive me and all of us.

إِذْ يُرِيكَهُمُ ٱللَّهُ فِى مَنَامِكَ قَلِيلاً وَلَوْ أَرَىٰكَهُمْ كَثِيرًا لَّفَشِلْتُمْ
وَلَتَنَـٰزَعْتُمْ فِى ٱلْأَمْرِ وَلَـٰكِنَّ ٱللَّهَ سَلَّمَ إِنَّهُ عَلِيمٌ بِذَاتِ
ٱلصُّدُورِ ۝ وَإِذْ يُرِيكُمُوهُمْ إِذِ ٱلْتَقَيْتُمْ فِى أَعْيُنِكُمْ
قَلِيلاً وَيُقَلِّلُكُمْ فِى أَعْيُنِهِمْ لِيَقْضِىَ ٱللَّهُ أَمْرًا كَانَ
مَفْعُولاً وَإِلَى ٱللَّهِ تُرْجَعُ ٱلْأُمُورُ ۝

(الأنفال ٨: ٤٣-٤٤)

*[Remember, O Muhammad], when Allah showed
them to you in your dream as few; and if He had
shown them to you as many, you [believers] would
have lost courage and would have disputed in the
matter [of whether to fight], but Allah saved [you
from that]. Indeed, He is Knowing of that within the
breasts. And [remember] when He showed them to
you, when you met, as few in your eyes, and He
made you [appear] as few in their eyes so that Allah
might accomplish a matter already destined. And to
Allah are [all] matters returned. (al-Anfāl 8:43-44)*

In these many ways, God grants me the choice to
proceed towards Him while keeping open the possibility
of guiding me. Pure material determinism is thus replaced
by a freewill that is conditioned either directly or indirectly by God through my context and interactions with
others. This partial freewill implies that it is impossible
for me to accurately anticipate the consequences of each
action I undertake. Hence, I need to be guided in order to

accomplish my goals, and that is precisely the role of the religious precepts: to guide me so that I can best achieve my purpose.

b. *The notions of good and evil*

Because the notions of "good" and "bad" are highly tainted by normative materialist worldviews, it is important to clarify their religious definitions. Following from the previous discussion on conditional freewill, the fact that God manages the course of history leads me to wonder why God, who calls Himself infinitely merciful and infinitely just, allows suffering on Earth. Indeed, God's mercy is God's prime quality:

(الفاتحة ١ : ١)

In the name of Allah, the Entirely Merciful, the Especially Merciful. (al-Fātiḥah 1:1)

Furthermore, I must accept that God is wise, and as such, the fact that He allows suffering is simply part of a greater, wiser plan.

أَلَيْسَ ٱللَّهُ بِأَحْكَمِ ٱلْحَـٰكِمِينَ

(التين ٩٥ : ٨)

Is not Allah the most just of judges? (al-Tīn 95:8)

I must then realize that, from a religious point of view, the notions of good and evil are separated from the joys and suffering that one feels. In general, pain and joy are immediate feelings, while good and bad refers to the long-term consequences of events.

كُتِبَ عَلَيْكُمُ ٱلْقِتَالُ وَهُوَ كُرْهٌ لَّكُمْ وَعَسَىٰٓ أَن تَكْرَهُواْ
شَيْـًٔا وَهُوَ خَيْرٌ لَّكُمْ وَعَسَىٰٓ أَن تُحِبُّواْ شَيْـًٔا وَهُوَ شَرٌّ
لَّكُمْ وَٱللَّهُ يَعْلَمُ وَأَنتُمْ لَا تَعْلَمُونَ ۝

(البقرة ٢: ٢١٦)

Fighting has been enjoined upon you while it is hateful to you. But perhaps you hate a thing and it is good for you; and perhaps you love a thing and it is bad for you. And Allah knows while you know not. (al-Baqarah 2:216)

God also says that He will test us with evil as well as good:

كُلُّ نَفْسٍ ذَآئِقَةُ ٱلْمَوْتِ وَنَبْلُوكُم بِٱلشَّرِّ وَٱلْخَيْرِ
فِتْنَةً وَإِلَيْنَا تُرْجَعُونَ ۝

(الأنبياء ٢١: ٣٥)

Every soul will taste death. And We test you with evil and with good as trial; and to Us you will be returned. (al-Anbiyā' 21:35)

Indeed, I do not know the future, and it may be that my current joy hides a greater subsequent suffering. Similarly, pain can be a source of subsequent comfort and joy. To illustrate this opposition, the Qur'an describes, for example, the encounter between Moses 🕮 and al-Khiḍr 🕮 during which God, through al-Khiḍr 🕮, protects certain individuals by inflicting them with hardship:[55]

أَمَّا ٱلسَّفِينَةُ فَكَانَتْ لِمَسَـٰكِينَ يَعْمَلُونَ فِى ٱلْبَحْرِ فَأَرَدتُّ

أَنْ أَعِيبَهَا وَكَانَ وَرَآءَهُم مَّلِكٌ يَأْخُذُ كُلَّ سَفِينَةٍ غَصْبًا

۝ وَأَمَّا ٱلْغُلَـٰمُ فَكَانَ أَبَوَاهُ مُؤْمِنَيْنِ فَخَشِينَآ أَن يُرْهِقَهُمَا

طُغْيَـٰنًا وَكُفْرًا ۝ فَأَرَدْنَآ أَن يُبْدِلَهُمَا رَبُّهُمَا خَيْرًا مِّنْهُ زَكَوٰةً

وَأَقْرَبَ رُحْمًا ۝ وَأَمَّا ٱلْجِدَارُ فَكَانَ لِغُلَـٰمَيْنِ يَتِيمَيْنِ فِى

ٱلْمَدِينَةِ وَكَانَ تَحْتَهُۥ كَنزٌ لَّهُمَا وَكَانَ أَبُوهُمَا صَـٰلِحًا فَأَرَادَ

رَبُّكَ أَن يَبْلُغَآ أَشُدَّهُمَا وَيَسْتَخْرِجَا كَنزَهُمَا رَحْمَةً مِّن رَّبِّكَ

وَمَا فَعَلْتُهُۥ عَنْ أَمْرِى ذَٰلِكَ تَأْوِيلُ مَا لَمْ تَسْطِع عَّلَيْهِ صَبْرًا ۝

(الكهف ١٨ : ٧٩–٨٢)

---

55. Moses 🕮, who was seeking Divine knowledge, asks permission to accompany al-Khiḍr 🕮 in the hope to learn from him. During their journey, al-Khiḍr 🕮 begins by damaging the boat of the poor people who welcomed them on board, then kills a child who was playing nearby his village and ended up undertaking the renovation of a wall, while they were in need of hospitality, without asking for any payment

"As for the ship, it belonged to poor people working at sea. So I intended to cause defect in it as there was after them a king who seized every [good] ship by force. And as for the boy, his parents were believers, and we feared that he would overburden them by transgression and disbelief. So we intended that their Lord should substitute for them one better than him in purity and nearer to mercy. And as for the wall, it belonged to two orphan boys in the city, and there was beneath it a treasure for them, and their father had been righteous. So your Lord intended that they reach maturity and extract their treasure, as a mercy from your Lord. And I did it not of my own accord. That is the interpretation of that about which you could not have patience." (al-Kahf 18:79-82)

The separation between the notions of good and bad, joy and pain, is also explicit in the case of the jogger, for example, who consciously inflicts on himself the pain of physical exercise in order to guarantee good physical health in the long term. The hope of a better future pushes one to go through difficulties and hurdles. Similarly, through the sacred texts, God asks one to dissociate the notion of good

---

in exchange. Moses 🙼, outraged and perplexed, shares his thoughts with al-Khiḍr 🙼. In response to the impatience of Moses 🙼, al-Khiḍr 🙼 decides to put an end to their company, but before doing that, he explains the reasons behind his actions. Once the justifications are given, we understand that al-Khiḍr 🙼 is, in a way, a personification of Divine will. Al-Khiḍr 🙼, by shedding light on God's mode of action, asks us to revisit our conception of good and evil.

from the joy one feels and evil from the suffering incurred. Separating these different notions implies that I cannot solely rely on my feelings to distinguish between right and wrong. I thus become dependent on what God declares to be good or bad. Since my objective in life is to worship God, I conclude that anything good is that which brings me closer to God and facilitates His adoration. Accordingly, anything bad is that which takes me away from His remembrance. On the one hand, the clear enunciation of what is good and bad, through the scriptures, prevents me from falling prey to harmful social constructions. On the other hand, such notions urge me to look beyond the immediate pleasures and seek long-term benefits, whether individual or societal. In this regard, we find that the Qur'an generically asks for the pursuit of justice:

﴿ وَهُوَ ٱلَّذِىٓ أَنشَأَ جَنَّـٰتٍ مَّعۡرُوشَـٰتٍ وَغَيۡرَ مَعۡرُوشَـٰتٍ وَٱلنَّخۡلَ وَٱلزَّرۡعَ مُخۡتَلِفًا أُكُلُهُۥ وَٱلزَّيۡتُونَ وَٱلرُّمَّانَ مُتَشَـٰبِهًا وَغَيۡرَ مُتَشَـٰبِهٍ كُلُواْ مِن ثَمَرِهِۦٓ إِذَآ أَثۡمَرَ وَءَاتُواْ حَقَّهُۥ يَوۡمَ حَصَادِهِۦ وَلَا تُسۡرِفُوٓاْ إِنَّهُۥ لَا يُحِبُّ ٱلۡمُسۡرِفِينَ ﴾

(الأنعام ١٤١:٦)

And He it is who causes gardens to grow, [both] trellised and untrellised, and palm trees and crops of different [kinds of] food and olives and pomegranates, similar and dissimilar. Eat of [each of] its fruit when it yields and give its due [zakah] on the day of its harvest. And be not excessive. Indeed, He does not like those who commit excess. (al-An'ām 6:141)

۞ إِنَّ ٱللَّهَ يَأْمُرُ بِٱلْعَدْلِ وَٱلْإِحْسَـٰنِ وَإِيتَآئِ ذِى ٱلْقُرْبَىٰ
وَيَنْهَىٰ عَنِ ٱلْفَحْشَآءِ وَٱلْمُنكَرِ وَٱلْبَغْىِ يَعِظُكُمْ
لَعَلَّكُمْ تَذَكَّرُونَ ۞

(النحل ١٦ : ٩٠)

Indeed, Allah orders justice and good conduct and giving to relatives and forbids immorality and bad conduct and oppression. He admonishes you that perhaps you will be reminded. (al-Naḥl 16:90)

يَـٰٓأَيُّهَا ٱلنَّاسُ إِنَّا خَلَقْنَـٰكُم مِّن ذَكَرٍ وَأُنثَىٰ وَجَعَلْنَـٰكُمْ
شُعُوبًا وَقَبَآئِلَ لِتَعَارَفُوٓا۟ إِنَّ أَكْرَمَكُمْ عِندَ ٱللَّهِ أَتْقَىٰكُمْ
إِنَّ ٱللَّهَ عَلِيمٌ خَبِيرٌ ۞

(الحجرات ٤٩ : ١٣)

O mankind, indeed We have created you from male and female and made you peoples and tribes that you may know one another. Indeed, the most noble of you in the sight of Allah is the most righteous of you. Indeed, Allah is Knowing and Acquainted. (al-Ḥujurāt 49:13)

And while these recommendations for justice are typically directed toward other human beings and animals, environmental justice is also indirectly addressed through the impact that the environment has on human life. We can, for example, see this concern for that which is "good for the health" in the following verse:

$$\text{وَكُلُوا۟ مِمَّا رَزَقَكُمُ ٱللَّهُ حَلَٰلًا طَيِّبًا وَٱتَّقُوا۟ ٱللَّهَ ٱلَّذِىٓ أَنتُم بِهِۦ مُؤْمِنُونَ ۝}$$

(المائدة ٥ : ٨٨)

And eat of what Allah has provided for you [which is] lawful and good. And fear Allah, in whom you are believers. (al-Māʾidah 5:88)

Accordingly, the recommendation goes beyond what is lawful (*ḥalāl*), but also encompasses what is actually wholesome (*Ṭayyib*)—beneficial for one's health and surrounding. I thus understand that to show respect to oneself, to other beings as well as to the rest of God's creation, is tantamount to fulfilling one of God's recommendations and is also a form of worship.

c. *The notions of success and failure*

Similarly, tainted by social norms and materialistic worldviews are the notions of success and failure. It is thus important to define them also in religious terms. Logically,

I should always choose what is good. However, as I am unable to probe the future and as my desires can be socially influenced, it becomes impossible to ensure that my actions always will lead to something good. Fortunately, the success and failure of my actions are also notions that religion clearly defines. As a general rule, God asks me to make an effort to evaluate my options and make the choice that seems best given my current understanding, and to leave the outcome to Him:

فَبِمَا رَحْمَةٍ مِّنَ ٱللَّهِ لِنتَ لَهُمْ وَلَوْ كُنتَ فَظًّا غَلِيظَ ٱلْقَلْبِ لَٱنفَضُّواْ مِنْ حَوْلِكَ فَٱعْفُ عَنْهُمْ وَٱسْتَغْفِرْ لَهُمْ وَشَاوِرْهُمْ فِى ٱلْأَمْرِ فَإِذَا عَزَمْتَ فَتَوَكَّلْ عَلَى ٱللَّهِ إِنَّ ٱللَّهَ يُحِبُّ ٱلْمُتَوَكِّلِينَ ۝

(آل عمران ٣ : ١٥٩)

So by mercy from Allah, [O Muhammad], you were lenient with them. And if you had been rude [in speech] and harsh in heart, they would have disbanded from about you. So pardon them and ask forgiveness for them and consult them in the matter. And when you have decided, then rely upon Allah. Indeed, Allah loves those who rely [upon Him]. (Āl ʿImrān 3:159)

Thus, God reserves for Himself the result of each action, and retribution will only be based on one's intention and effort.[56] More specifically, God promises success to the one who makes an effort to purify himself, avoids corruption, believes, does good deeds, enjoins the truth and perseveres in doing so:

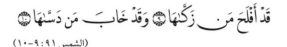

(الشمس ٩١: ٩-١٠)

He has succeeded who purifies it, and he has failed who instils it [with corruption]. (al-Shams 91:9-10)

إِنَّ ٱلْإِنسَٰنَ لَفِى خُسْرٍ ۝ إِلَّا ٱلَّذِينَ ءَامَنُوا۟ وَعَمِلُوا۟ ٱلصَّٰلِحَٰتِ وَتَوَاصَوْا۟ بِٱلْحَقِّ وَتَوَاصَوْا۟ بِٱلصَّبْرِ ۝

(العصر ١٠٣: ٢-٣)

Indeed, mankind is in loss, except for those who have believed and done righteous deeds and advised each other to truth and advised each other to patience. (al-ʿAṣr 103:2-3)

Since the fulfilment of each of these recommendations cannot be measured objectively, success becomes a subjective, individual and immaterial notion, which is based

---

56. Actions are judged only by their intentions, as reported in the following *ḥadīth*: "Umar Ibn al-Khaṭṭāb ﷺ narrated: 'I heard Allah's Messenger ﷺ saying, "The reward of deeds depends on the intentions and every person will get the reward according to what he has intended."'" (*Ṣaḥīḥ al-Bukhārī*, Vol. 1, Book 1, *ḥadīth* 1.)

on one's relationship with God, independent of any external factor. This detachment from any material measuring stick (salary, social status, popularity rating, material goods) allows one to overcome disappointment when a project does not lead to the expected results. For example, if I do not obtain the job I applied for, I am asked to believe that not getting that job is better for me in the long run. And this posture will allow me to focus on other projects. Furthermore, this notion of success allows one to detach oneself from peer pressures and social constructions. To define success in relation to God liberates us from the notion of success as perceived by the masses or as promoted by the media. Such a notion of success, because it is freed from material measures, promotes altruism and makes prevail the respect of moral rather than material gain. I find, for example, this connection between success and detachment, in the call to prayer (*adhān*), when the believer is successively called to perform the actual prayer (*ṣalāh*) and then to success (*falāḥ*), as if the detachment provided by the prayer is a victory over the material world.

d. *Section summary*

In summary, I reviewed some of the concepts that form the basis of an Islamic worldview. Just as scientific theories require the scientist to revisit his intuitive conception of space and time, Islam requires its follower to review the notions of freewill, good, evil, success and failure. And it is by linking these notions to God directly that religion helps to overcome the trials of life and liberates from material constraints. Once these conceptions are redefined and the internal logic is put in place, I can now explore the benefits of practising this religion, as it will be discussed in the following section.

5. A useful religion

The previous evaluation of the historicity of the texts, the evaluation of their relevance (scientific, as far as I am concerned) and the underlying logic of the proposed worldview, helps me build trust in the texts: it reassures me that the material is sound and coherent with itself. With such trust, I am now ready to explore the usefulness of the different religious practices. The idea is that, even for a scientific theory which is deemed to be "true," if it has no application in our everyday life, it risks being dismissed by the general public (cf. relativity and quantum mechanics). Similarly, I take that even if a religion is perceived as true, it must be useful in order to be appreciated and practised by the general public. I understand that the ultimate purpose of religion goes beyond material gains: its objective is to bring us closer to God. To this aim, Islam, as the last "religion of the Book," builds on the notion of love that is prevalent in Christianity, but also stays true to the rigorous nature of Judaism. While love is an integral part of Islam, because it is essential to build a relation with God and His creation, I will only deal with the benefits that one can derive from adhering to the rituals. At first sight, prayer, fasting, abstinence from certain foods, and other religious practices, seem to curtail rather than promote satisfaction. However, the spiritual elevation which is promoted by the

Qur'an and exemplified by the Prophet ﷺ should guarantee an improvement of my psychological state. Furthermore, an improved psychological state is expected to ensue, in the medium term, in an improved material situation. Surely, my objective in life should not be to burden myself physically or psychologically with the pursuit of material gains. But I argue that taking advantage of this religion, including material advantages, is a mark of faith. Likewise, asking for guidance in every mundane matter can be a proof of reliance on God and, thus, of faith. In this chapter I will therefore expose some of the psychological and material benefits generated by adhering to religious views and practices.

a. *Positivity*

As argued in the first chapter of this book, long term satisfaction is found by keeping some distance from materiality. In this aim, prayer, for example, invites me to suspend my daily material occupations. The recommended alms (*zakāt*) literally asks me to let go of some of my material possessions. Fasting invites me to become aware of my needs and excesses. The pilgrimage disconnects me temporarily from my daily life to get as close as possible to God by enacting Judgement Day. The different food restrictions invite me to make morals prevail over satiety—respect for the animal, preservation of physical and intellectual health). I thus appreciate that each of these religious practices help me distance myself from this material world. As said, material goods are fated to decay: our bodies age and belongings wear out. Thus, by considering these goods as means (to use them for something) rather than goals (to collect them for the sake of it), I protect myself from all their weaknesses. It is this detachment, added to a notion of intangible success established in relation to God, that enables me to overcome material difficulties and helps me reinterpret life's challenges as an opportunity to get closer to God. Such an attitude helps me to overcome, for example, the disappointment of losing a precious object such as my high-end computer (which has worryingly become the primary mean through which I interact with the world). Religion teaches me that this computer is not an end in itself, but that its value comes from its utility. This material detachment thus gives space to a reliance on the Divine. Accordingly, religious practices invite me to build trust in God: trust that God is infinitely good and just and that He reserves the best for each of us. For example, if my computer stops working, it must be for a greater good and I shall find this utility in another device. Hence, the ability to re-evaluate my goals while maintaining hope for a better future, the ultimate future being Paradise, allows me to keep up my morale in the face of material loss and disappointment. As long as I act according to Divine guidance, to the best of my ability and understanding, I am invited to see all outcomes as benefits and opportunities, regardless of the material gain obtained or loss incurred. This is how worship helps me maintain a positive view of the world.

b. *Agency*

In this section I argue that religious practices also help me build agency—that they make me a more effective actor in my society. I have already discussed how religious practices help me reconsider the material objects as vehicles rather than as objectives in themselves. Similarly, the acts of worship are not objectives, but means to get closer to God.[57] The physicality of rituals thus becomes a mere material expression of a spiritual conviction: I believe and, thus, I act accordingly. Indeed, the Prophet ﷺ said in multiple occasions that faith requires appropriate actions.[58] Likewise, the Qur'an often juxtaposes belief (*Īmān*) with good deeds (*al-aʿmāl al-ṣāliḥāt*) in order to prompt the believer to act upon it and implement his ideals:

$$\text{إِنَّ ٱلْإِنسَٰنَ لَفِى خُسْرٍ ۝ إِلَّا ٱلَّذِينَ ءَامَنُواْ وَعَمِلُواْ}$$
$$\text{ٱلصَّٰلِحَٰتِ وَتَوَاصَوْاْ بِٱلْحَقِّ وَتَوَاصَوْاْ بِٱلصَّبْرِ ۝}$$

(العصر ١٠٣ : ٢–٣)

Indeed, mankind is in loss, except for those who have believed and done righteous deeds and advised each

---

57. This notion of intimacy with God through religious practices can be seen from the following narration: Abū Hurayrah ؓ narrated that Allah's Messenger ﷺ said, "Allah said: 'the most beloved things with which My slave comes nearer to Me is what I have enjoined upon him; and My slave keeps on coming closer to Me through performing *Nawāfil* (praying or doing extra deeds besides what is obligatory) till I love him, so I become his sense of hearing with which he hears, and his sense of sight with which he sees, and his hand with which he grips, and his leg with which he walks." *Ṣaḥīḥ al-Bukhārī*, Vol. 8, Book 76, *ḥadīth* 509.

58. For example: The Prophet ﷺ said, "None of you will have faith till he wishes for his brother what he likes for himself." (*Ṣaḥīḥ al-Bukhārī*,

other to truth and advised each other to patience.
(*al-'Aṣr* 103:2-3)

It is interesting to note that Islam insists on precision in basic religious practices. For example, the prayer is performed at particular times of the day and night and is composed of a succession of well-defined postures during which I am invited to reflect on specific parts of the texts. The *zakāt* is a predefined percentage taken from one's wealth. The fasting of Ramadan is a well-defined practice, which takes place only during a fixed period of the year. The pilgrimage also consists of a series of specific acts carried out in a defined order and during specific days of the year. Thus, Islam links religious conviction not only to any given good actions, but to well-defined and concise actions. The stronger my faith, the more attentive I am vis-à-vis the details of these actions. With this understanding, religious practices serve as a daily training to act upon my convictions: from the idea to its careful implementation. And since Islam informs actions in all spheres of life, I am expected to be meticulously active in all spheres of life. Moreover, by promoting a worldview that is informed by revelation rather than based on social norms, Islam

---

Vol. 1, Book 2, *ḥadīth* 13.) And also: "Between man and polytheism and unbelief is the abandonment of *salat*."(*Ṣaḥīḥ Muslim*, Book 1, *ḥadīth* 147.

"The Muslim is the one from whose hand and tongue the Muslims are safe." *Ṣaḥīḥ Muslim*, Book 1, *ḥadīth* 65

prompts me to challenge these social norms and strive for a more just society.

c. *Efficiency*

In this section I argue that, although religious practices take time to be performed and perfected, they nonetheless help me to be more efficient and, thus, they help me to better manage my time. Indeed, the different religious practices (prayer, fast, the poor-due, pilgrimage) are prescribed for specific time of the day, week or year. They literally punctuate and structure my life. The five daily prayers, in particular, because they are prescribed at different times during the day (dawn, noon, afternoon, dusk and night), force me to compartmentalize my time. The prayers then serve as points of reference for the beginning and end of each of my daily activities. The prayer, because it is an effort of meditation and reconnection with the Divine, helps me to take a step back from my current activities and asks me to re-evaluate them. Moreover, because the prayer is one of the most meritorious acts of worship, it implies that all other occupations should either facilitate the prayer or be subordinated to it. I am thus invited to re-evaluate and put all these other actions on a priority scale: are these occupations worth delaying my prayers? Are these occupations facilitating my prayer or helping me pray better? By inviting me to this type of reflection, each religious practice, besides being meritorious acts of worship, help me re-evaluate my material and spiritual goals, whether daily, weekly, monthly or annually. And it is through such prioritization of activities that I am able to benefit most of every moment. Furthermore, the physical constraints implied by the religious practices serve as a training for controlling my desires and regain control of my own self. For example, during each station of the prayer, I refrain from any movements or mental wandering. During the pilgrimage, some usual acts are no longer allowed. Fasting, more specifically, involves dietary and behavioural constraints that will help me regulate my appetites, reactions and, ultimately, character. All these efforts to achieve control over my self, along with the prioritization of my goals and activities, will inevitably make me more effective.

d. *Summary*

In summary, religious practices serve as a daily training regime to promote and maintain a certain distance vis-à-vis the materiality of this world. This detachment allows me to focus on the utility of objects or occupations rather than on the objects or occupation themselves. It is this material detachment associated with the idea of a good and just God, as well as the hope of a better future, that help me overcome material loss. Ultimately, this detachment prepares me for the unavoidable consequences of aging and death. But for time being, by associating conviction with action, religious practices serve as a training for enacting my ideals. And if these ideals are influenced by the religious precepts of love and respect for the people around me, I will see myself actively building a more socially just society. Furthermore, by punctuating the day, week, month and year, religious practices make me attentive to the passing of time and help me avoid falling into the routine of life through inviting me to regularly re-evaluate each action. Finally, the material constraints required by religious practices help me regain control over my desires. It is this self-control associated with the prioritization of my actions that will make me a more effective member of society.

So far, I have been judging the religious practices based on the material benefits they provide. And I did so to argue that, even from a materialist point of view, religion does fulfil the condition of being useful. However, I bear in mind that, from an Islamic point of view, the material benefits generated and maintained by religious practices are themselves only vehicles for spiritual elevation. I would however argue that looking forward to any material benefits that may ensue from following religious practices is also an expression of faith. It is to be convinced that whatever God asks me to do is inherently beneficial in all spheres of life. Accordingly, I am allowed to look forward to these material benefits to increase in my devotion.

6. Chapter summary

In this chapter, I reviewed the different intellectual steps necessary to accept a scientific theory: origin, relevance, and utility. I then applied these same criteria to Islam in order to show that being religious is as rational as being a scientist. Indeed, if a religion fulfils the same conditions as the ones that are necessary to accept a scientific theory, then there are no objections, scientifically speaking, to refrain from accepting this religion as a valid worldview. In this aim, I appreciate, in the first instance, that I can still evaluate the historical origin of Islam. This historicity helps me build trust in the sacred texts: the Qur'an and the Prophetic narrations. And it is these texts that I then examine to evaluate the message in terms of its relevance. Contrary to public opinion, I see complementarity between this religion and the current scientific view of the world. And like a scientific theory, Islam has its supporting arguments, it provides a worldview, it has its own logic and own benefits that make it a coherent and rational whole. The fact that I am able to evaluate Islam with scientific rigour might not be a mere coincidence. It most probably reflects the fact that scientific method was developed under Islamic influence by religious thinkers such as Ibn al-Haytham, al-Bayrūnī and Ibn Sīna. I must emphasise that I am not trying here to scientifically prove the truth of Islam, but simply to demonstrate its rationality. As a matter of fact, I have still not found in the sciences any direct, self-sufficient or absolute proof for the existence of God. I have only found evidences. By evidences, I refer to phenomena which, when taken individually, can support multiple theories at once. By absolute proof, I refer to an argument that is strong enough to support the theory on its own. With regard to Islam, I do not know of any such proof from within the sciences.

However, there is plenty of evidence, and when I combine all the evidences together, whether it is the ordering of the universe, the chemistry of life, the preservation of the sacred texts, the life of the Prophet ﷺ, the scientific relevance of the message, to name a few, the whole picture becomes clear. Supported by scientific reasoning, in today's scientific age, the act of faith is no longer a weakness of the mind, but the fruit of an educated choice.[59]

59. I, of course, keep in mind that it is ultimately God who guides to Islam. Hence, when I say that Islam is my choice, I mean that God allowed me and facilitated me the path to Islam. See section III.4.a) on conditional freewill. Again, my goal here is to emphasize the rationale behind such a choice.

IV

LIMITS AND DANGERS OF PURELY RATIONAL THOUGHT

Until now, I have used scientific reasoning to justify a religious worldview. However, this tool, which is called rationality, only allows me to build trust in the texts and accept the existence of a world that goes beyond this material realm. In my search for Truth and ultimate happiness, it is mostly to my feelings that I will be attentive and, to that end, scientific reasoning is of little use. Indeed, scientific reasoning is only effective with what can be "datafied," meaning things that can be empirically measured. Science cannot probe what exists beyond this material world. Reason thus paves the way but is not sufficient to undergo this spiritual journey. Rationality is necessary but it has its limits, and it is this limitation that I will highlight in the first section of this chapter. This will be followed by a discussion about the different ways we perceive the world, whether material or immaterial. And I will finish with a discussion on the use of the imagination in this spiritual quest.

1. Mathematics and programming as divine languages.

Isn't it impressive that the physical laws of our world can be so well described by mathematics? A man-made and universal language which, by means of numbers and equations, makes it possible to model the interactions between objects: a pebble that rolls can be described in terms of energy and momentum, which ought to be conserved; sunlight becomes an electromagnetic wave that is radiated; a meal becomes a number of kilocalories to be burned following the rules of calorimetry. Wasn't Einstein looking for a unifying equation that God would have used to create the whole of the universe? Every physical phenomenon can be translated into mathematical equations, and every equation can be translated into algorithms for efficient solving.

As far as computing is concerned, programming is a language with a well-defined grammar and vocabulary. It allows me to control machines and communicate with information repositories on which our lives are forever linked. Who is still able to go about his or her life without using the internet? Our means of communications, transport and even consumption are governed by computer programs. Financial institutions, in particular, are the most demanding and hire the best physicists, engineers and statisticians who are able to programme the most complicated equations. Maths and programming have become universal languages that are used to understand and exploit this world. My concern is that these languages are devoid of subjectivity, compassion or poetry: who has seen the operating system of his computer written in prose? Who has ever gotten a homework where the instruction is to demonstrate a theorem using equations that rhyme? Although the definition of prose or rhymes in mathematical and programming terms can be discussed, my argument is that these languages are primarily used to achieve material efficiency and not to express emotions. These languages are used for optimisation, precision and reliability, for example which are necessary qualities in our modern age. But they hardly speak to the soul, or let emotion speak out like poetry, music or the other arts do.

What I find worrying, on the one hand, is that these mathematical and programming languages won't allow me to express my feelings and thus develop my sentience. Consequently, I fear that the constraints of these languages lead to a blindness of the heart, which itself might hinder spiritual experiences. On the other hand, it also becomes much easier to hide behind numbers and act upon emotions that are otherwise shunned by society when publicly displayed, such as greed and hate. It is, for example, unfortunately common to see in our own workplaces how numbers shape loyalties and recognitions.

Let's now imagine a universal language, accepted by all, but which does not allow the expression of feelings and, thus, does not favour sentience to the point where it becomes nearly impossible to connect with the Divine. Imagine the state of a society that is governed by such mode of communication and, consequently, whose constituents are emotionally illiterate. With such disconnection from the Divine, where would morality finds its grounding, if not from God? What morality would this society live by? Can morality emanate from pure science or numbers? Which objectives would this society be running towards? The little I know about human nature tells me that this society would be prone to self-destruction. It is certainly easy to blame maths and programming for the ills of the contemporary world. My goal is not to free myself from responsibilities and blame instead such and such people or institutions for pushing forward a worrisome reliance on information technologies. My goal is not to eradicate such technologies, but rather to check that my morality, sensitivity, and relationship with the world and with God are not limited to emotionless series of numbers and equations.

2. At the edges of rationality: experiencing the Divine

In this section, I argue that our sentience might be the most direct way to experience the Divine. I have already described in the second chapter that we experience the world through our senses: hearing, touch, sight, taste, smell, which are mediated through organs (ears, skin, eye, tongue, nose). Each of these organs translates the stimuli into ionic signals which are then sent to the brain. If I consider the latter as the material support of my conscience, I deduce that all the information received from my organs are biased since the stimuli are processed and transmitted before being integrated by the brain. Hence, this information is processed before it becomes part of my consciousness. Consequently, the perception that I have of the material world is not a direct experience but a mediated one that, by definition, can be distorted and even illusory. For example, when the retina of one's eye is damaged (for example due to laser burn, as is the case with some of my colleagues working on high-power lasers), the damaged retina will send an incomplete image to the brain, compared to the one sent by the healthy eye. At first, one will see a hole in the field of vision of the affected eye, and over time the brain will compensate for this hole. It turns out that the brain fills the lack of information by extending the image surrounding the damaged area, so that the person is no longer inconvenienced. For instance, if one were to look at a lush forest, the hole would appear green; if one were to read a book with black characters written on a white paper, the hole appears grey. This phenomenon, called "neural adaptation," shows that my physical senses can be deceived according to my needs, whether these needs are conscious or not.

To illustrate further this point about false consciousness, I recall, for instance, playing with my son and looking for a small wooden stick to fix his toy. I had found in his supply box what looked like the tip of wooden Chinese chopsticks. I took it in my hand and carved it into the desired shape. I was going back and forth between the toy and the knife I had in the other hand, until it had the proper shape. It was at this point I detached the curved piece from the rest of the stick. And it is only after I had finished fixing the toy that I realized that I had curved the handle of one of my son's paint brushes. It might seem trivial, but during the whole process I was convinced I was holding a simple wooden stick, and somehow my mind was oblivious to the shape and feel of the metal and hairs of the paint brush. My mind had supressed all of these stimuli.

Beyond our senses, another way to perceive the world is through emotions such as joy, love, fear, that are felt in specific situations. These feelings, unlike the five physical senses, do not require the intermediation of an organ other than the nervous system itslef. They can certainly be triggered by signals from one's organs, like feeling joy when seeing something pleasing, but are not constrained by, or solely dependent on, these organs. For example, looking repetitively at the same pleasing sight might not result in the same sense of joy every single time. I thus consider these feelings as the most direct and authentic experiences I can have of the world, because they require a minimum of physical intermediaries. Accordingly, emotions could be the most direct way to experience the Divine, while living in the material world. I would also argue that our ability to listen to our feelings, like any other physical senses, can be developed through training and practice. Scientists today are trying to explain and rationalize emotions by talking about hormones and other neurotransmitters. Although we are capable to chemically manipulate emotions via, for example, antidepressants and other drugs, the generation of an emotion remains unexplained from a purely material point of view. Indeed, feelings are not palpable and thus cannot be measured or scanned objectively.

In discussing emotions, we are flirting with another limit of the current sciences. Rationality or scientific reasoning is curtailed by a wall made of unanswered questions. What are emotions? What is consciousness? Why this world? What is my purpose? Scientific reasoning can only take me up to that wall, and it is Prophecy that will allow me to climb over this wall and find answers by guiding my intuition towards a religious interpretation of the world. After comforting my faith using scientific reasoning, I thus turn to my emotions and perceptions, which are the most direct ways to experience this world, to dare to experience the Divine.

3. The use of imagination

After having defined sentience as the most direct way to experience the Divine, I here suggest the use of imagination as a means to develop sentience. For example, when I stand and get ready to pray, I say *Allāhu akbar* ("God is greater") to initiate my prayer, but nothing changes in appearance. The room in which I stand remains the same. And yet, the simple act of uttering these words while intending to pray is supposed to project me in front of God. While I am reciting verses of the Qur'an, I am supposed to be speaking to Him, with Him listening and answering back to me. How, then, is it possible to reconcile the fact that nothing changes materially, while I am supposed to stand before God? I can only reconcile the two if I believe in an invisible world beyond the material one. And the only tool I currently have at hand to bridge this gap is my imagination.

Let me give you an anecdote that illustrates the use of imagination in religion. It was a meditation experience organized by my friend Max, a Buddhist monk from the Tibetan centre of Rabten Choeling in Mont-Pèlerin (canton of Vaud, Switzerland), during an inter-faith workshop. The session consisted of imagining Buddha's love in the form of a light that gradually fills our hearts and bodies and then overflowing and spreading to all the people around us, on earth and beyond. This experience made me realize that imagination, instead of being considered a delusion, is in fact a common tool to developing spirituality. As a Muslim, I can then use revelation to guide this imagination. Accordingly, in order to gain concentration in my prayers, I picture the verses that I am reciting. Indeed, the highly graphical descriptions of the Qur'an are perfectly suited to such an exercise. Hence, while scientific reasoning justifies a theistic vision of the world, I will use guided imagination to depict the surrounding unseen world. And with conviction, these mental representations become realisations which, ultimately, help me feel His presence.[60]

---

60. I must mention here that to use imagination to develop spirituality has already been proposed and even criticized. I refer, for example, to René Guénon in his *The Crisis of the Modern World*, who would consider me to be far away from the traditional spirit of the mystics or, in other words, to be deluded. However, following Muhammad Iqbal's *The Reconstruction of Religious Though in Islam*, if I am to use modern tools to develop myself spiritually, I see no better or more efficient way than imagination to increase in concentration while in prayer and to develop my sentience.

4. Chapter summary

Mathematics and programming languages are considered the ultimate languages of rationality. Their strength lies in their lack of subjectivity. Constant and universal, they are ubiquitous to our daily life: I wake up with an alarm programmed on my mobile; I go to work using public transport whose flow is regulated by a software. At work, I am either on my laptop or in the lab using software to acquire, process and analyse data. In a shop, I pay using electronic money. I use social media to interact with family and friends. Even my prayer times are computed. At every instant, my life is facilitated directly or indirectly by a programme code or a server, somehow, somewhere. These languages dictate the way I interact with the world and, consequently, they condition my vision of the world.

As I said, the strength of programming languages lies in their lack of subjectivity, and it is this very strength that limits the expression of my emotions. I thus worry that my interactions with the world and with others, because they are facilitated by such limiting tools, are also confined and formatted to the pursuit of efficiency, interest, and material profit. How convenient indeed are these visually appealing but emotionless numbers and flow-charts to hide our greed and inability to stand up for human dignity. Going back to my spiritual journey, I initially based it on scientific reasoning because it provides me with arguments that support the veracity of Revelation: it helps me build trust in the Prophet ﷺ and his message. Scientific reasoning thus confirmed for me a theistic vision of the world.

But scientific reasoning does not allow me to experience this unseen world. It is then through sentience, helped by an imagination that is informed by Revelation, that I will be able to detach myself from a purely materialist worldview and experience the Divine.

CONCLUSION

In this book, I expounded upon some aspects of my spiritual journey. I recognize that the questions I asked myself and the answers I found were certainly a product of my Western materialist socialisation. Due to the current condition of globalisation, I fear that these Western con-cerns are be-coming normative beyond the Western world and across cultures. As such, I believe that this book can help others who, like me, were at the verge of either getting caught into scientific dogmatism or needed some scientific grounding to strengthen their belief. Indeed, in the society in which I grew up, religion was like an old painting fixed on the wall. I used to pass in front of it every day. It nicely filled the space, but no one remembered who put it there, nor what it really meant. As a young boy, I was too busy with my toys and video games to bother about it. Science, by contrast, because it created my toys and my videogames, and also because it promised me a lucrative future, was a lot more attractive and valuable than religion. Consequently, when I was implicitly asked by society to make a choice between the two, science or religion, I didn't think twice. I pursued a scientific career and, as a result, I developed a liking for science and learned to see the world through scientific lenses. As a result of this socialisation, I approached Islam with the same scientific liking and felt the need to evaluate this religion scientifically. During my studies, I realised that, while science provided space for religiosity, Islam's worldview coincided with the current scientific understanding of the world. As a Muslim scientist, I am now able to evolve in harmony between rationality and spirituality: the former validating the latter, the latter completing the former. My scientific reasoning gives me the peace of mind and the confidence to persevere in religion and even to dare to seek a spiritual experience. If a spiritual experience is to be sought, I will seek it through the realisation of revelation-led imagination and sentience. In return, religious conviction gives me the strength to fully live this life, to have agency, to overcome challenges, and to pursue ideals. To conclude with a metaphor, I imagine faith as a tree. Its roots are the evidence all the signs that point towards God. When taken individually, each root might seem fragile and vulnerable, but when taken in their entirety, the whole root system represents a sturdy support for the trunk of faith. Within this picture, scientific reasoning is like the stake that serves as a support for my tree of faith to grow strong. This stake, because it is based on a common logic, withstands the bad weather, which illustrates the tests and doubts of this life. By leaning on this stake, the tree will be able to grow branches, leaves and fruits of spirituality. These adornments of faith do fluctuate with the seasons, but the whole tree is expected to grow stronger every year until, who knows, the stake might not be of any use anymore... And God knows best.

Appendix

EVOLUTION

E volution is one of the most delicate and con-troversial topics of our time. For many it rep-resents the decisive argument for choosing religion or atheism. Indeed, through the theory of evolution, mankind is, for the first time in History, capable of explaining its presence on Earth solely using material arguments and assumptions without resorting to any Divine intervention. Consequently, people have used this theory as an argument to adopt a purely materialistic vision of the world. As God is no longer needed in their view, they have classified religion itself as an evolutionary relic and an outdated vision of the world. However, I showed above that the physical explanation of phenomena does not negate its Divine nature. I further argue that the theories of evolution and creation, from an Islamic point of view, are not necessarily contradictory. Towards in this aim, I will first review the scientific position: its development, strengths and weaknesses. Then I will review the religious texts relating to the creation of man, to finally show that the Islamic vision of creation has much more in common with the theory of evolution than is commonly perceived. In other words, I suggest that the Islamic story of human creation can also be read in light of the theory of evolution.

i. Supporting evidences for the theory of evolution

I admit that every time I walk in to a paleontological museum, I am amazed by the morphological similarities throughout the vast majority of animal species displayed: such as the skull, ribcage, limbs. From the snake to the turtle, passing by the whale, the similarities are undeniable. Do you know, for example, that the turtle's shell is simply an extension of its vertebrae? The palaeontological register is in fact the expression of a common genetic base. Indeed, all known living organisms share a genetic code (DNA) made of the same nucleic acids, which works according to the same processes: replications, transcription and translation. It is the genetic similarities between species that are used to draw phylogenetic trees, these beings the diagrams that show species deriving from previous ones. As a matter of fact, a good number of protein complexes are shared between all animals and even plants. For example, one finds in both plants and animals a small molecule called adenosine triphosphate (ATP). This protein is used to transport energy (stored as a chemical bond) from one end of the body to the other. As such, it is a universal energy currency. It is produced by a biological power plant called

ATP synthase: a molecular three-stroke rotary engine. It turns out that every living organism has a counterpart of this ATP synthase. With such similarities between the most varied species, it would be an act of "bad faith" not to imagine that all living organisms are connected in some ways and, consequently, that they might have a common origin.

ii. An incomplete and simplistic theory

Similarities between species, however, are not a sufficient criterion for establishing the existence of a law of kinship between them. It is after observing genetic modifications within species that, by extrapolation, one expects major genetic rearrangements to lead to the emergence of a new species. In fact, from a purely materialist perspective, one simply has no other arguments to explain the appearance of new species. The argument of the common ancestor is tempting and personally pleasing to the mind (which could be a reminiscence of my indoctrination). But, from a scientific point of view, it does not rely on any direct proof. To give an example, all diamonds are made of an identical crystalline structure. This similarity, however, does not imply kinship, but simply the result of similar geological processes. Yet, we have already mentionned that modern scientific theories do not require direct proofs to be validated. This last point is here important and will be discussed later.

Regarding the theory of evolution as it is taught in school: life would have started with a spontaneous assembly of organic matter in the "primordial soup" to give birth to the original organism(s). Indeed, amino acids have been found in meteorites. The heat, humidity and other properties of our Earth at its early stage would have favoured the constitution of more complex organic material (through Fischer-Tropsch-type of reactions), produced at random. In other words, it is similar to taking random metal blocks, to shake them well in a bag and to hope that, with a little luck and time, they will shape and assemble themselves to form a working engine. Through this metaphor, it becomes obvious that, even with a few billion years, this theory, which advocates for the "spontaneous" appearance of a functional cell capable of living, growing and reproducing, remains extremely simplistic in view of the current understanding of science (physics, chemistry, thermodynamics). The theory itself is based on the assumption that, with enough time, the conditions favourable to life will necessarily appear somewhere, somehow. Indeed, in terms of probabilities, everything is possible, even throwing a dice that does not stop on one of its faces but in balance on one of its vertices. Another and more likely hypothesis (given how little we know of our own physical world) is that life has emerged as a result of physico-chemical forces and interactions that are still unknown. In either case, whether this original cell is the result of a sequence of highly improbable events or unknown processes, it amounts to a belief.

After the creation of an original organism, or colonies of organisms, the theory of evolution suggests that a species arises from a previous one as a result of genetic mutations. However, we have never witnessed a genetic rearrangement such that it allows the appearance of a new species. There are indeed a growing number of interesting studies on bacterial populations that can be used to support some sort of evolution across species. However, all these studies, given the large number of bacteria involved, are based on statistical models and the data is interpreted, by default, in terms of evolutionary biology. In other words, it is equivalent to assuming the truth of the theory that is to be proven. The conclusions are inherently biased. But beyond the biased rules upon which this field is based, it is the definitions of key terms that is still required. While looking for speciation, the definition of a species itself is debatable: how much different must the subsequent generation be with respect to the original one in order to be considered a "new" species? And surely, depending on the chosen definition, the fossil record as well as the bacterial colonies in the lab can be either devoid of or filled with intermediary species.

One may also argue that, in order to be valid, a theory must be "falsifiable," which refers to its ability to be proven wrong. In the case of evolution, however, this condition cannot be fulfilled as the theory pertains to speciation events that are expected to have already taken place a long time ago and which are not expected to be witnessed in natural conditions during a single lifetime. Similarly, while studying speciation, we are not looking at the emergence of a single new species, but at statistical changes and patterns, oftentimes across hundreds of different species. Accordingly, the conclusions are model dependent. And if the data persistently resists to be fitted by the model, it is only the model that will be discarded, but not the underlying theory. The only way to disprove this theory therefore is to witness speciation events that do not involve any known genetic processes. Such alternative speciation process, according to our current knowledge, would be considered a miracle. In other words, in order to prove or disprove evolution, given the current state of knowledge, one has to either travel back in time and witness thousands (if not millions) of years of subsequent genetic modifications, or witness some sort of spontaneous speciation. In either case, a miracle is necessary. Interestingly, modern theories do not seem to be restricted to this falsifiability principle. On the contrary, to strictly apply the falsifiability principle would render the scientific endeavour impossible, as no theory ever fully explains all data available. The falsifiability principle is useful to choose between competing theories, but to this day evolution does not know any scientific alternatives.

With respect to the process of speciation via random genetic mutation, from what we have been witnessing so far in complex organisms, none has yet resulted in tangible results, but it was always associated to some degeneration and premature death. It is true that genetically modified organisms (GMOs) can make a plant or animals more resistant to certain environmental factors or force them to express one of their characteristics disproportionately (size, morphology, growth rate, etc.), but it is often at the expense of other characteristics (taste, smell, nutritional value, etc.). Actually, of all the molecules that I had the chance to study, none had a unique function. A chlorophyll molecule, for example, can sometimes be used as an antenna to absorb light (in a light harvesting complex), sometimes it is used as a gateway to block the passage to another molecule (within a cytochrome $b_6 f$), and sometimes it is used to accept or supply an electron (in a photosystem I and II). The same chlorophyll molecule plays a different role depending on the context in which it is placed. Modifying the expression of a single constituent in an organism therefore amounts to changing the context in which the other molecules perform. And, in turn, the functions of these other molecules are likely to be altered. In view of the complexity and fragile balance of this "chemistry of life," I like to think that if one is the result of an evolutionary process, as described above, then the thesis of a random reorganization of the genetic material is no more convincing than that of an orchestrated genetic reorganization. Whether this orchestration is the result of the Divine or unknown scientific laws, my stand is not to dismiss one or the other, but to show that, given our current understanding, evolution is closer to a belief than to an empirical scientific law.

iii. A theory that is evolving

The idea of evolution emerged from observing the similarities between living species as well from the study of the fossil record. With time, more living species are being genetically sequenced, the fossil record keeps growing and, in turn, the theory keeps being refined. The geological analysis of strata shows for example the diversity of crustacean species over (geological) time. Based on these studies, one can trace and date the different massive extinctions (i.e. simultaneous disappearance of many species), as well as the periods of proliferation (i.e. sudden appearances of multiple new species), like the famous Cambrian explosion. These geological analyses have, for example, led researchers to dismiss the idea of a progressive evolution and adopt that of a punctuated equilibrium theory. The latter theory states that the appearance of new species is the result of modifications which take place during a geologically short period of time before stabilizing, with no further genetic modifications. Note that the notions of time such as "simultaneous," "sudden," "explosion" and "short," from a geological point of view, can still involve tens of millions of years.

Another recent development of this theory is that hot spring environments have been found to be favourable to the spontaneous polymerisation of RNA (i.e. without the need of any molecular machinery).[61] We still don't know how spontaneous RNA leads to a protocell, but it is a first step. In other words, scientists are looking for ways to explain the emergence of life through purely material means, and they do make progress. I thus emphasize that the theory of evolution is itself evolving and we must expect future adaptations.

---

61. See Professor Bruce Damer's origin of life theory at: https://extended evolutionarysynthesis.com/the-hot-spring-hypothesis-for-the-origin-of-life-and-the-extended-evolutionary-synthesis/

iv. What the Qur'an says

For this section, let's imagine that humans are the result
of a Divine reorganization of the genetic code. The goal is
thus to reconcile this vision with the creation of man, and
more precisely of Adam 🕊, as it is stated in the Qur'an.
Indeed, the Qur'an says that:

- a. Adam 🕊 was the first human being to have been
  created.
- b. God created Adam 🕊 following *"kun fa-yakūn"*

إِنَّ مَثَلَ عِيسَىٰ عِندَ ٱللَّهِ كَمَثَلِ ءَادَمَ خَلَقَهُۥ مِن
تُرَابٍ ثُمَّ قَالَ لَهُۥ كُن فَيَكُونُ ۝

(آل عمران ٣ : ٥٩)

*Indeed, the example of Jesus to Allah is like that of
Adam. He created Him from dust; then He said to
him, "Be," and he was. (Āl 'Imrān 3:59)*

ɪ.   In the particular case of Adam 🕊, God created him:

FROM DUST

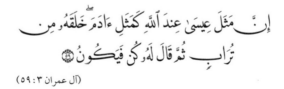

إِنَّ مَثَلَ عِيسَىٰ عِندَ ٱللَّهِ كَمَثَلِ ءَادَمَ خَلَقَهُۥ مِن
تُرَابٍ ثُمَّ قَالَ لَهُۥ كُن فَيَكُونُ ۝

(آل عمران ٣ : ٥٩)

Indeed, the example of Jesus to Allah is like that of Adam. He created Him from dust; then He said to him, "Be," and he was. (Āl 'Imrān 3:59)

FROM CLAY

إِذْ قَالَ رَبُّكَ لِلْمَلَـٰٓئِكَةِ إِنِّى خَـٰلِقٌۢ بَشَرًا مِّن طِينٍ ۝ فَإِذَا سَوَّيْتُهُۥ وَنَفَخْتُ فِيهِ مِن رُّوحِى فَقَعُوا۟ لَهُۥ سَـٰجِدِينَ ۝ فَسَجَدَ ٱلْمَلَـٰٓئِكَةُ كُلُّهُمْ أَجْمَعُونَ ۝ إِلَّآ إِبْلِيسَ ٱسْتَكْبَرَ وَكَانَ مِنَ ٱلْكَـٰفِرِينَ ۝ قَالَ يَـٰٓإِبْلِيسُ مَا مَنَعَكَ أَن تَسْجُدَ لِمَا خَلَقْتُ بِيَدَىَّ ۚ أَسْتَكْبَرْتَ أَمْ كُنتَ مِنَ ٱلْعَالِينَ ۝ قَالَ أَنَا۠ خَيْرٌ مِّنْهُ خَلَقْتَنِى مِن نَّارٍ وَخَلَقْتَهُۥ مِن طِينٍ ۝

(ص ٣٨: ٧١-٧٦)

[So mention] when your Lord said to the angels, "Indeed, I am going to create a human being from clay. So when I have proportioned him and breathed into him of My [created] soul, then fall down to him in prostration." So the angels prostrated - all of them entirely. Except Iblees; he was arrogant and became among the disbelievers. [Allah] said, "O Iblees, what prevented you from prostrating to that which I created with My hands? Were you arrogant [then], or were you [already] among the haughty?" He said,

*"I am better than him. You created me from fire and
created him from clay." (Ṣād 38:71-76)[62]*

OUT OF CLAY FROM AN ALTERED BLACK MUD

وَلَقَدْ خَلَقْنَا ٱلْإِنسَـٰنَ مِن صَلْصَـٰلٍ مِّنْ حَمَإٍ مَّسْنُونٍ ۝
وَٱلْجَآنَّ خَلَقْنَـٰهُ مِن قَبْلُ مِن نَّارِ ٱلسَّمُومِ ۝ وَإِذْ قَالَ رَبُّكَ
لِلْمَلَـٰٓئِكَةِ إِنِّى خَـٰلِقٌ بَشَرًا مِّن صَلْصَـٰلٍ مِّنْ حَمَإٍ مَّسْنُونٍ
۝ فَإِذَا سَوَّيْتُهُ وَنَفَخْتُ فِيهِ مِن رُّوحِى فَقَعُوا۟ لَهُۥ سَـٰجِدِينَ
۝ فَسَجَدَ ٱلْمَلَـٰٓئِكَةُ كُلُّهُمْ أَجْمَعُونَ ۝ إِلَّآ إِبْلِيسَ أَبَىٰٓ
أَن يَكُونَ مَعَ ٱلسَّـٰجِدِينَ ۝ قَالَ يَـٰٓإِبْلِيسُ مَا لَكَ
أَلَّا تَكُونَ مَعَ ٱلسَّـٰجِدِينَ ۝ قَالَ لَمْ أَكُن لِّأَسْجُدَ
لِبَشَرٍ خَلَقْتَهُۥ مِن صَلْصَـٰلٍ مِّنْ حَمَإٍ مَّسْنُونٍ ۝

(الحجر ١٥: ٢٦-٣٣)

*And We did certainly create man out of clay from an
altered black mud. And the jinn We created before
from scorching fire. And [mention, O Muhammad],
when your Lord said to the angels, "I will create a
human being out of clay from an altered black mud.
And when I have proportioned him and breathed*

---

62. For the creation of Adam 🕊 from clay, see also (*al-Aʿrāf* 7:12 and
Banī Isrāʾīl 17:61).

into him of My [created] soul, then fall down to
him in prostration." So the angels prostrated - all of
them entirely, Except Iblees, he refused to be with
those who prostrated. [Allah] said, O Iblees, what
is [the matter] with you that you are not with those
who prostrate?" He said, "Never would I prostrate
to a human whom You created out of clay from an
altered black mud." (al-Ḥijr 15:26-33)

2. As for life and man in general, God created them:

FROM WATER

وَٱللَّهُ خَلَقَ كُلَّ دَآبَّةٍ مِّن مَّآءٍ فَمِنْهُم مَّن يَمْشِى عَلَىٰ بَطْنِهِۦ
وَمِنْهُم مَّن يَمْشِى عَلَىٰ رِجْلَيْنِ وَمِنْهُم مَّن يَمْشِى عَلَىٰٓ أَرْبَعٍ يَخْلُقُ
ٱللَّهُ مَا يَشَآءُ إِنَّ ٱللَّهَ عَلَىٰ كُلِّ شَىْءٍ قَدِيرٌ ۝

(النور ٢٤:٤٥)

*Allah has created every [living] creature from water.
And of them are those that move on their bellies,
and of them are those that walk on two legs, and of
them are those that walk on four. Allah creates what
He wills. Indeed, Allah is over all things competent.*
(al-Nūr 24:45)[63]

---

63. For creation from water, see also (al-Anbiyā' 21:30 and al-Furqān
25:54).

FROM AN EXTRACT OF DISDAINED LIQUID

ٱلَّذِىٓ أَحْسَنَ كُلَّ شَىْءٍ خَلَقَهُۥ ۖ وَبَدَأَ خَلْقَ ٱلْإِنسَـٰنِ مِن

طِينٍ ۞ ثُمَّ جَعَلَ نَسْلَهُۥ مِن سُلَـٰلَةٍ مِّن مَّآءٍ مَّهِينٍ ۞

(السجدة ٣٢: ٧–٨)

*Who perfected everything which He created and
began the creation of man from clay. Then He made
his posterity out of the extract of a liquid disdained.*
(al-Sajdah 32:7-8)[64]

FROM DUST

وَمِنْ ءَايَـٰتِهِۦٓ أَنْ خَلَقَكُم مِّن تُرَابٍ ثُمَّ إِذَآ أَنتُم

بَشَرٌ تَنتَشِرُونَ ۞

(الروم ٣٠: ٢٠)

*And of His signs is that He created you from dust;
then, suddenly you were human beings dispersing
[throughout the earth].* (al-Rūm 30:20)[65]

---

64. For creation from a vile water, see also (al-Mursalāt 77:20).
65. For creation from dust, see also (al-Kahf 18:37, al-Ḥajj 22:5, Fāṭir 35:11
and al-Mu'min 40:67).

FROM AN EXTRACT OF CLAY

وَلَقَدْ خَلَقْنَا ٱلْإِنسَـٰنَ مِن سُلَـٰلَةٍ مِّن طِينٍ ۝

(المؤمنون ٢٣ : ١٢)

And certainly did We create man from an extract of clay. (al-Mu'minūn 23:12)

FROM CLAY

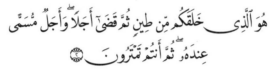

(الأنعام ٦ : ٢)

It is He who created you from clay and then decreed a term and a specified time [known] to Him; then [still] you are in dispute. (al-An'ām 6:2)[66]

FROM STICKY CLAY

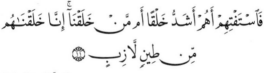

(الصّافات ٣٧ : ١١)

Then inquire of them, [O Muhammad], "Are they a stronger [or more difficult] creation or those [others]

---

66. For creation from clay, see also (*al-Sajdah* 32:7).

We have created?" Indeed, We created men from sticky
clay. (al-Ṣāffāt 37:11)

FROM CLAY LIKE THAT OF POTTERY

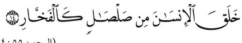

(الرحمن ٥٥: ١٤)

He created man from clay like [that of] pottery. (al-
Raḥmān 55:14)

FROM EARTH

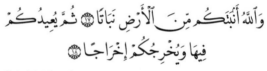

(نوح ٧١: ١٧-١٨)

And Allah has caused you to grow from the earth
a [progressive] growth. Then He will return you
into it and extract you [another] extraction. (Nūḥ
71:17-18)[67]

FROM A SPERM DROP

مِن نُّطْفَةٍ خَلَقَهُۥ فَقَدَّرَهُۥ ۝

(عبس ٨٠: ١٩)

---

67. For creation from earth, see also (Hūd 11:61 and al-Najm 53:32).

From a sperm-drop He created him and destined for him; ('Abasa 80:19)[68]

FROM A BLOOD CLOT/CLINGING SUBSTANCE

اقْرَأْ بِٱسْمِ رَبِّكَ ٱلَّذِى خَلَقَ ۝ خَلَقَ ٱلْإِنسَٰنَ مِنْ عَلَقٍ ۝

(العلق ٩٦ : ١-٢)

Recite in the name of your Lord who created – Created man from a clinging substance. (al-'Alaq 96:2)[69]

Let's evaluate each of these points:

1. Adam ﷺ is known as the first man to have appeared on Earth. It is interesting to note that, from an evolutionist point of view, the theory requires the existence of a common ancestor. The two points of view, religious and evolutionist, agree on this notion of universal kinship.

2. As for "*kun fa-yakūn*," which translates as "Be! And it is.", at first sight, the expression indicates a notion of brevity that directly conflicts with an evolution that began a few billion years ago. On the contrary, I would argue that "*kun fa-yakun*" can accept a notion of evolution over time. Indeed, what is brief for God, who is free from of our concept of space and time, is not neces-

---

68. For creation from sperm, see also (*Banī Isrā'īl* 17:4, *al-Kahf* 18:37, *al-Ḥajj* 22:5, *al-Mu'minūn* 23:13, *Fāṭir* 35:11, 77 and *al-Qiyāmah* 75:37).

69. For creation from a blood clot/clinging substance, see also (*al-Qiyāmah* 75:38).

sarily brief for us, humans, who are constrained by this space-time. To support this hypothesis, let's look at the comparison that God makes between the conception of Jesus 🕊 and that of Adam 🕊. In both cases, He says that it was enough to say "*kun*":

$$\text{إِنَّ مَثَلَ عِيسَىٰ عِندَ ٱللَّهِ كَمَثَلِ ءَادَمَ خَلَقَهُۥ مِن تُرَابٍ ثُمَّ قَالَ لَهُۥ كُن فَيَكُونُ}$$

(آل عمران ٣: ٥٩)

Indeed, the example of Jesus to Allah is like that of Adam. He created Him from dust; then He said to him, "Be," and he was. (Āl 'Imrān 3: 59)

However, the mother of Jesus 🕊, Mary (🕊), had a determined gestation period during which she went in exiled until she gave birth:

$$\text{۞ فَحَمَلَتْهُ فَٱنتَبَذَتْ بِهِۦ مَكَانًا قَصِيًّا ۞}$$

(مريم ١٩: ٢٢)

So she conceived him, and she withdrew with him to a remote place. (Maryam 19:22)

Furthermore, the body of Jesus 🕊 also took some time to develop: embryonic development, gestation, birth, growth, etc. But none of these stages are explicitly mentioned. These omissions give to the reader the feeling that it took only a brief instant. This relativity of time is also mentioned explicitly in the Qur'an when God indicates that one of His days corresponds to thousands of our years:

وَيَسْتَعْجِلُونَكَ بِالْعَذَابِ وَلَن يُخْلِفَ ٱللَّهُ وَعْدَهُۥ وَإِنَّ يَوْمًا عِندَ رَبِّكَ كَأَلْفِ سَنَةٍ مِّمَّا تَعُدُّونَ ۝

(الحج ٢٢:٤٧)

And they urge you to hasten the punishment. But Allah will never fail in His promise. And indeed, a day with your Lord is like a thousand years of those which you count. (al-Ḥajj 22:47)

Thus, with respect to the creation of Adam 🕮 and Jesus 🕮, the mention of "*kun fa-yakūn*" doesn't necessarily implies brevity as we experience it but indicates His omnipotence and the ease with which He created us.

3-4. As for our creation from water, dust, clay, etc., one may wonder what God means by these terms:

▶ Do they correspond to a figure of speech or to a sort of simplified language that would have been more relevant to a population that had limited scientific understanding of the material world and its physical laws?

▶ Or did God create the template of a man using different materials, just like the potter makes a vase, and He then gave it life?

As far as I know, the sciences cannot explain the passage from an inanimate object to a living being. For example, the transformation of the staff of Moses 🕮 into a snake is scientifically enigmatic. Similarly, during the development of the foetus, the passage from a cluster of cells to a living human being is still clinically undetermined. The same uncertainty exists with the appearance of consciousness. In fact, whether man was created from a clay figure or through evolution from an original cell, current science is unable to explain the passage from inert matter to life.

From another point of view, the fact that life is said to originate from different materials (water, dust, earth, and different types of clay) implies that these verses cannot be taken literally, because each of these verses would contradict each other. A certain level of interpretation is thus necessary, and we are left to decide which interpretation to opt for. Interestingly, the different materials mentioned in the creation of man are related to each other: the dust mixed with water gives mud as well as the different types of clay. The transition from one to the other implies a reorganisation of the elements. Thus, the mention of water, dust, mud and clay implies different stages in the creation of man. These steps allude to an evolution or a progressive transformation of the raw materials. I therefore argue that the two visions of the world, religious, through the Qur'an, and scientific, through the theory of evolution, can agree on this notion of process and reworking of the constitutive elements that make the building block of life (from dust, and all what it contains, to amino acids to a fully functional organism).

In another passage, the Qur'an does mention both types of creation sequentially: first from clay, then from sperm, then to an embryo and until death:

وَلَقَدْ خَلَقْنَا ٱلْإِنسَـٰنَ مِن سُلَـٰلَةٍ مِّن طِينٍ ۞ ثُمَّ جَعَلْنَـٰهُ نُطْفَةً فِي قَرَارٍ مَّكِينٍ ۞ ثُمَّ خَلَقْنَا ٱلنُّطْفَةَ عَلَقَةً فَخَلَقْنَا ٱلْعَلَقَةَ مُضْغَةً فَخَلَقْنَا ٱلْمُضْغَةَ عِظَـٰمًا فَكَسَوْنَا ٱلْعِظَـٰمَ لَحْمًا ثُمَّ أَنشَأْنَـٰهُ خَلْقًا ءَاخَرَ فَتَبَارَكَ ٱللَّهُ أَحْسَنُ ٱلْخَـٰلِقِينَ ۞ ثُمَّ إِنَّكُم بَعْدَ ذَٰلِكَ لَمَيِّتُونَ ۞ ثُمَّ إِنَّكُمْ يَوْمَ ٱلْقِيَـٰمَةِ تُبْعَثُونَ ۞

(المؤمنون ٢٣: ١٢–١٦)

And certainly, did We create man from an extract of clay. Then We placed him as a sperm-drop in a firm lodging. Then We made the sperm-drop into a clinging clot, and We made the clot into a lump [of flesh], and We made [from] the lump, bones, and We covered the bones with flesh; then We developed him into another creation. So blessed is Allah, the best of creators. Then indeed, after that you are to die. Then indeed you, on the Day of Resurrection, will be resurrected. (al-Mu'minūn 23:12-16)

If this verse refers to an evolutionary process, from clay to the emergence of homo-sapiens, then it has omitted the few billion years of evolution that passed between the creation of the primordial cell (from clay) to the creation of human semen. Note that in this specific verse, the intermediate stages between the creation of the embryo up to the death of men are not described either. To omit some of the intermediary steps of a process is in fact a common practice in the Qur'an. For example, when the stories of the Prophets such as Joseph ﷺ, Moses ﷺ, and Jesus ﷺ are told, the Qur'an overlooks important periods of their physical and mental development. It is thus common for the Qur'an to be silent about certain developmental stages, regardless of their physical importance and duration. By omitting the intermediate steps, God focuses our attention on the moral lessons that are to be derived from the texts.

By mentioning water, dust, earth and clay, I understand that we ultimately come from earth and water. I take the mention of these various elements as a reminder of our humble origin. Indeed, even by reducing life to a reorganization, at the atomic level, of the elements and to a succession of physiological processes, the passage from an inert matter that one tramples underfoot to an intelligent being will always be bewildering regardless of the theory adopted.

If I now accept the possibility of an evolutionary process, and read the texts in the light of these assumptions, I would argue that many verses would actually make more sense. For example, when God is asking us to travel the lands to witness the beginning of creation:

أَوَلَمْ يَرَوْاْ كَيْفَ يُبْدِئُ ٱللَّهُ ٱلْخَلْقَ ثُمَّ يُعِيدُهُۥٓ إِنَّ ذَٰلِكَ عَلَى ٱللَّهِ يَسِيرٌ ۞ قُلْ سِيرُواْ فِى ٱلْأَرْضِ فَٱنظُرُواْ كَيْفَ بَدَأَ ٱلْخَلْقَ ثُمَّ ٱللَّهُ يُنشِئُ ٱلنَّشْأَةَ ٱلْآخِرَةَ إِنَّ ٱللَّهَ عَلَىٰ كُلِّ شَيْءٍ قَدِيرٌ ۞

(العنكبوت ٢٩ : ١٩ـ٢٠)

Have they not considered how Allah begins creation and then repeats it? Indeed that, for Allah, is easy. Say, [O Muhammad], "Travel through the land and observe how He began creation. Then Allah will produce the final creation. Indeed Allah, over all things, is competent." (al-'Ankabūt 29:19-20)

Why would God ask me to travel the land to witness how creation began? If God refers to the creation of men by a male and a female, then I don't have to go anywhere since it is sufficient to look at my own family. Similarly, if God refers to the seasonal growth of plants, I only need to look at the surrounding gardens and crops. If God refers to the creation of mankind or the origin of life via some supernatural means that are contrary to our current physical sciences (e.g. the shaping of clay by God's hand and the blowing of life into it), then there is nothing to witness from a scientific point of view, except perhaps the absence of scientific evidence. This verse would however make sense if God was referring to the origin of life via processes that (1) we are able to study and (2) which are not obvious unless we travel the land. These two conditions immediately bring to my mind Charles Darwin's journey on the H.M.S. Beagle, which allowed him to develop the first draft of the theory of evolution. Hence, I see through this verse the hint that the creation is a field worth studying and that it requires in-depth investigations, which is the role played today by evolutionary biologists.

v. Concordance with the *Ḥadīth*s

Concerning the Prophetic narrations, the margin of interpretation is more limited because the words are more explicit. The narrations pertaining specifically to the creation of Adam 🕮 report that:

1. he was created from different earths.[70]
2. he was created during the last moments of creation.[71]
3. he was about 30 metres tall.[72]

---

70. "[...] Abu Musa al-Ash'ari 🕮 narrated that the Messenger of Allah 🕮 said: "Indeed Allah Most High created Adam from a handful that He took from all of the earth. So the children of Adam come in according with the earth, some of them come red, and white and black, and between that, and the thin, the thick, the filthy, and the clean." *Jāmiʿ al-Tirmidhī*, Vol. 5, Book 44, *ḥadīth* 2955.

71. Abū Hurayrah 🕮 reported that Allah's Messenger 🕮 took hold of my hands and said: "Allah, the Exalted and Glorious, created the clay on Saturday and He created the mountains on Sunday and He created the trees on Monday and He created the things entailing labour on Tuesday and created light on Wednesday and He caused the animals to spread on Thursday and created Adam (peace be upon him) after 'Asr on Friday; the last creation at the last hour of the hours of Friday, i.e. between afternoon and night." *Ṣaḥīḥ Muslim*, Book 39, *ḥadīth* 6707. Friday being considered the last day of the creation.

72. Abū Hurayrah 🕮 narrated that the Prophet 🕮 said: "Allah created Adam, making him sixty cubits tall. [...] People have been decreasing

First of all, lets remind ourselves that the Prophet ﷺ was aware of certain aspects of the past, present and future of his community, and that he had to convey this knowledge using a language that was understood by his contemporaries. Hence, it would not have been proper for the Prophet ﷺ to speak in scientific terms to a population that did not have scientific knowledge or vocabulary. How could he (and why would he) talk about genetic rearrangement of DNA to a population that was not even aware of what a cell is? Similarly, when Abraham ﷺ asks God to strengthen his heart by showing him how He brings the dead back to life, God does not dwell on a scientific explanation but merely proves His omnipotence by concrete experience. God simply asks Abraham ﷺ to cut into pieces four birds that will eventually come back to him, alive:

وَإِذْ قَالَ إِبْرَٰهِـۧمُ رَبِّ أَرِنِى كَيْفَ تُحْىِ ٱلْمَوْتَىٰ قَالَ أَوَلَمْ تُؤْمِن قَالَ بَلَىٰ وَلَـٰكِن لِّيَطْمَئِنَّ قَلْبِى قَالَ فَخُذْ أَرْبَعَةً مِّنَ ٱلطَّيْرِ فَصُرْهُنَّ إِلَيْكَ ثُمَّ ٱجْعَلْ عَلَىٰ كُلِّ جَبَلٍ مِّنْهُنَّ جُزْءًا ثُمَّ ٱدْعُهُنَّ يَأْتِينَكَ سَعْيًا وَٱعْلَمْ أَنَّ ٱللَّهَ عَزِيزٌ حَكِيمٌ ۝

(البقرة ٢: ٢٦٠)

And [mention] when Abraham said, "My Lord, show me how You give life to the dead." [Allah] said,

---

in stature since Adam's creation." *Ṣaḥīḥ al-Bukhārī*, Vol. 4, Book 55, *ḥadīth* 543. Note that sixty cubits is approximately equal to ninety feet or to thirty meters.

"Have you not believed?" He said, "Yes, but [I ask] only that my heart may be satisfied." [Allah] said, "Take four birds and commit them to yourself. Then [after slaughtering them] put on each hill a portion of them; then call them - they will come [flying] to you in haste. And know that Allah is Exalted in Might and Wise." (al-Baqarah 2:260)

Likewise, I assume that the Prophet ﷺ needed to stay at the level of understanding of his community. This standpoint thus allows me to approach the narrations with an extra layer of interpretation.

1. Concerning the creation from a mixture of different earths giving birth to the different physical traits, I understand that by "earth," Adam ﷺ was created from the minerals present on our planet, then formed with multiple phenotypes that would be expressed or supressed in himself and his descendent depending on their living conditions. Even today, the reference, in everyday language, to one's homeland often implies a behavioural aspect. Words like "earth" and "colour" can therefore refer to a specific social context and character traits which, in scientific terms, could refer to epigenetics.

2. Regarding the time of the creation of Adam ﷺ in relation to the rest of the universe, religions and science agree that man is one of the last species that appeared on Earth, in the very last moments of its history.

3. Concerning the size of Adam ﷺ, it turns out that the existence of human giants is not scientifically accepted; on the contrary, the archaeological remains (dwellings

and tools) point to ancestors of similar size as ours. But these archaeological remains are limited in the sense that they only correspond to selected artefacts belonging to communities that have already achieved some levels of technological advancements. It is nevertheless interesting to note that the fossil record shows that many ancestors of present animals were much larger in prehistoric times: rats, horses, camels, elephants, lizards, etc.[73] It seems that among these species, only the smaller members have survived over time. A similar tendency for the human species could correspond to the description made by Prophet Muhammad ﷺ when he says: "People have been decreasing in stature since Adam's creation."[74] As for the number itself, "sixty cubits," I have already mentioned that numbers might have cultural connotations. I would also like to reiterate that:

- ▶ The fossilization process requires very peculiar environmental conditions.
- ▶ The fossils record therefore represent only a tiny sample of the populations present at a specific time and location.

---

73. See the article of P.S. Martin. Prehistoric Overkill: The Global Model. Chapter 17 from the book of P.S. Martin and R.G. Klein (1984), *Quaternary Extinctions: A Prehistoric Revolution*, Tucson: University of Arizona Press, pp. 354-403. The primary purpose of this article is to link the extinction of large animals, who lived in the Pleistocene epoch, with the presence of man; and to do this, the authors enumerate the members of this "megafauna" by specifying their current descendants, their geography and their period of life.

74. See the footnote 69. Ṣaḥīḥ al-Bukhārī, Vol. 4, Book 55, ḥadīth 543.

- ▶ The ritual burial accelerates the process of degradation, which makes fossilization almost impossible.
- ▶ The absence of fossils does not mean that a specific species did not exist, but simply that no remains have been found.

Thus, if we admit the existence of an ancestor of *homo sapiens* of much greater size, these last arguments could explain why we have never found any such skeleton. The same arguments also explain the scarcity of the fossil record. In addition, the Prophetic narrations indicate that Adam ﷺ initially lived in Paradise before descending to Earth. To make these narratives coincide with the current scientific understanding of the origin of man, I could further discuss the term "Adam": does it correspond to the physical body deprived of any soul or with soul? Does it refer to a particular individual or to a community? Was Adam's ﷺ Paradise the same as the one we are aiming for? Was the fall of Adam ﷺ physical or is it a metaphor to indicate a different state of consciousness? All this to say that there is room left to make both worldviews coincide.

vi. Ending notes

Between the rejection of the Prophetic narrations that are contrary to current scientific understanding and their dogmatic acceptance, I prefer to explore the interpretative margin of the texts and of the sciences. The goal is to find common grounds and engage in a more constructive discussion. Note that I have here interpreted the texts to fit current evolutionary theories. However, my goal is not to mould the religious as if it were dependent on current scientific understanding. My goal is simply to demonstrate that the texts can accept an evolutionary reading. My goal is to prove that current scientific theories, whatever their validity, do not justify rejection of the religious texts. On the contrary, creationism, as it is described in the texts, has many more similitudes than contradictions with the current theory of evolution.

In summary, despite its limitations, I find the theory of evolution pleasant as it highlights a developmental process as well as the existence of a relationship between each living organism, as implied by the religious texts. This theory reinforces the idea of an "Adam," in other words, of an original individual, who is at the origin of the human species. It also puts into perspective the uniqueness of life by pointing to our humble material origin. From a scientific point of view, this theory is still incomplete in the sense that it is currently based on simplistic arguments, such as spontaneous apparition of a proto-cell, and apparent similarities between species, and unfounded extrapolations—that speciation is driven by random mutations). Consequently, with all its shortcomings, to consider the theory of evolution as an established law is a leap of faith in and of itself. However, evolution remains the dominant paradigm within scientific circles, certainly because, from a scientific point of view, there are currently no alternatives. From a religious point of view, I maintain that the interpretative margins of the texts admit a so-called theistic evolution.[75] I further argue that some verses can be more easily interpreted in light of this theory.

Finally, I find it interesting to see that all ancient religions depict a cosmogony that involves some kinds of direct Divine interactions. As such, this creationist understanding of the origins of humankind must have been a contemporary theme during the Prophet's ﷺ time. Islam does not depart from this trend as it also alludes to similar creationist ideas when the Qur'an mentions the moulding of Adam out of dirt and his birth following "Be! And it is." To read the text from a creationist perspective would then be intuitive and even comforting to the Prophet's ﷺ contemporaries. Indeed, I can imagine that if the Revelation gave details about natural progression from dirt to bacteria, to fishes to monkeys to humans, such a clash of paradigms would have prevented people from adhering to the faith. But the texts only allude to creationism and, as demonstrated above, also accept an evolutionary reading. And it is in this multiplicity of readings that I see miracles. As a scientist, I find miraculous the fact that the same verses, which pertains to material descriptions of the world, remain relevant across the ages and across the changes in scientific paradigms.

---

75. From a practical point of view, this theistic view of evolution would simply imply the 'Hand of God' is behind each and every step, irrespective of their scientific comprehension. Hence, it does not change the science, but it helps to stay true to the religious creed, which is to see God behind every object and events, or, in other words, to take every object and event as an indicator that points to God.